CUTE, QUAINT, HUNGRY AND ROMANTIC

Cute, Quaint,
Hungry and Romantic

THE AESTHETICS
OF CONSUMERISM

BY
DANIEL HARRIS

BASIC

BOOKS

A Member of the Perseus Books Group

Copyright © 2000 by Daniel Harris

Published by Basic Books,
A Member of the Perseus Books Group

A CIP catalog record for this book is available from the Library of
Congress
ISBN 0-465-02848-9

designed by Rachel Hegarty

FIRST EDITION
00 01 02 03 / 10 9 8 7 6 5 4 3 2 1

To John MacLaren

CONTENTS

INTRODUCTION

My life is suspended above an abyss of ignorance. Virtually nothing I own makes sense to me. What happens when I flick on my light switch? Why does my refrigerator keep my food cold? How does my answering machine record the voices of my friends? When I delete a paragraph on my word processor, what makes it disappear and where in the world does it go? In the interest of saving time, as well as out of pure laziness, I, like most people, have deliberately chosen to leave these questions unanswered, preferring to remain unenlightened rather than to undertake a lengthy—and, more likely than not, futile—education in thermoelectric currents, vector fields, and ionic conduction. I live quite happily hemmed in on all sides by an impenetrable wall of technological riddles. I do not know how the toilet flushes or why water comes out of my faucet or what makes my Hoover suck up dust, and yet—to my credit—I continue to flush, wash my dishes, and vacuum, entirely unaware of *how* I am doing these things.

The same ignorance, I would argue, pertains to the aesthetic features of our daily environments, to the decorations on our teaspoons and cereal boxes, to the metallic snowflakes embossed on our freezer doors, or to the hallucinatory poetry of our screen savers, gratuitous details that we ignore as conscientiously as the cathode ray tubes in our television sets and the motherboards in our PCs. We no longer truly see our world, know how it looks, let alone how it works. Exposed to more images than we can possibly appreciate, we have developed a kind of collective aesthetic unconsciousness, a psychic realm of forgetfulness that, much as the Id serves as the repository for many of the formative experiences of infancy, serves as a storehouse for faint memories of the extraneous designs on trash cans, jelly jars, and milk cartons. And yet the Disney characters who flip cartwheels on our mouse pads or the glittery speckles and veins of marble on the tiles of our linoleum floors play a small role in helping us to navigate successfully among the scientific conundrums in which we live.

In the chapters that follow, I attempt to recover the repressed aesthetic data of our lives; to make this vast archive of subliminal images accessible to conscious analysis; and to remove the mental obstructions, the inveterate habits of inattentiveness, that prevent us from seeing how carefully even the most insignificant of our possessions have been designed. We are trained to look for art in only one location, on the walls of museums and galleries, whereas art is—and always has been—entirely indiscriminate in its choice of venue, appearing on ketchup bottles, subway passes, digital alarm clocks, placemats, heating pads, and thermoses. Wallowing in the seemingly random sensory data of my life, I will travel out of museums and into kitchens and bathrooms, where I will sightsee in my own backyard, studying the aesthetic features of toothpaste tubes and Kotex advertisements, prime-time sit-coms and toilet bowl cleaners, Hollywood goofball comedies, and the breakfast menus at greasy spoons.

This psychic voyage into the aesthetic unconsciousness places the refuse of consumerism under a microscope and concentrates on minutiae, on the uses of the useless, the significance of the insignificant: How has the ring of the telephone changed in the last twenty years? Why are bottles of cleaning fluids frequently transparent? What ever happened to the fenders of cars? Is there a reason that the buttons on calculators and TV remote controls are made of soft, clickless rubber? If we like stains on old furniture, why do we abhor them on clothing? How has feminism modified the image of the naked bather in soap advertisements? Why do lovers on greeting cards always walk on beaches? Who decided that food commercials should never mention hunger? Why do stuffed animals seldom have paws? Do recently scrubbed sinks and bathtubs have distinct smells, as the manufacturers of cleaning products would have us believe? When did bad posture and messy hair become de rigueur for the contemporary fashion model? Why has the teddy bear gained so much weight in the course of the twentieth century? When were hippies replaced by yuppies in natural foods commercials? Why are cars frequently shown off-road in car advertisements?

Each chapter defines one broad principle that governs the appearance of popular culture, of movies and Saturday morning cartoons, of posh designer clothing stores on Madison Avenue and Piggly Wigglys in suburban Tallahassee malls. The aesthetic road map that emerges, while admittedly incomplete and based on my own idiosyncratic interests, delves into the ways in which the ostensibly purposeless appearance of consumerist debris affects us psychologically, even if it serves no pragmatic function in helping us to operate a computer or cook with a convection oven. My walking tour through this visual labyrinth is not intended as an historical treatise on economics, class relations, or political theory, nor as an authoritative description of a single dominant aesthetic, but merely as a thread to lead us through the beaten tracks and wandering byways of our preferences and appetites. We live in a landscape characterized by extreme eclecticism, if not outright incoherence: Rusty cowbells stand side-by-side in our kitchens with streamlined, chrome-plated Cuisinarts; we display cute Teletubbies and Beanie Babies on our office desks next to dolls that spew expletives when we poke their tummies; we watch *Gone With the Wind* one week and *Do the Right Thing* the next; we wear battered Reebok running shoes while swinging glamorous Prada bags, and high-waisted granny dresses while sporting cool black shades. Rather than denying this chaos and identifying the "system" behind the nearly inexhaustible menu of tastes available to us, I have a more modest aim, that of recreating the world of consumerism in all of its contradictions, of bringing it to life and capturing its immediacy.

To understand the effects of free enterprise on the average person, it is important to do more than simply record the solemn pronouncements of Allan Greenspan and keep abreast of volatile fluctuations in business cycles and the intricacies of 401(k)s and offshore tax shelters. It is necessary to examine consumerism on the level on which the consumer actually experiences it: on the visceral level of the senses, of our bodies, from the point of view of the hand reaching for the soup can on the store shelf, the ears listening to the boom box broadcasting the sounds of a cool, refreshing soft drink splashing into a frosted glass, and the eyes fixed on the screen of the multiplex as the *Titanic* sinks and cars careen into fruit stands. Shoppers and moviegoers do not know capitalism from the standpoint of Hegelian dialectics and Althusserian Marxism, of plummeting prime interest rates and spurts of growth in the Gross National Product, but rather from the perspective of the sensations caused by the vibrant colors of labels, the enticing rhetoric on packages, and the dewy-eyed beauty of actresses in romantic comedies. What happens when we come face to face with a product, recognize its jingle, confront the billboard plastered with an advertisement for the latest Eddy Murphy caper or the bus laminated from bumper to bumper with a gigantic image of a Coke can? It is this moment of engagement, of seduction, the very instant that our neurons begin to fire, that I attempt to recreate in my evocation of the false sensuality of the marketplace, which at once overwhelms us with its dazzling pyrotechnics, its captivating sights and sounds, and, paradoxically, deprives us of actual physical pleasure.

Jeremiads against consumerism (and mine is unabashedly a jeremiad) are generally flawed in two ways. First, their contemptuous appraisals of the ugliness and vulgarity of capitalism are in fact simply covert attacks on the bad taste of the lower classes, mean-spirited burlesques that function as a backhanded form of self-congratulation, a way of bolstering the author's confidence in his own refinement. What's more, the typical objection to consumerism is highly moralistic, based on an unaccountably dour disapproval of creature comforts, on the conviction that the materialism of the marketplace detracts from our spiritual and intellectual well-being, that shopping is a vicious pastime for the simple-minded, and that politically responsible people take pleasure only in books and ideas and eschew narcissistic luxuries that inevitably seduce the righteous from the straight-and-narrow. While I make no secret of my dislike of consumerism or, for that matter, of my fascination with its exuberance, I have made valiant efforts to rise above both snobbery and censoriousness. At the same time, it would be disingenuous of me not to confess at the outset that I share my generation's—and, I suspect, my readers'—prejudices against conspicuous consumption and recoil from a society that revolves so maniacally around acquisition, even while I recognize that I am indebted to it—indeed, that my very survival depends on it. It is perhaps inevitable, therefore, that I will upon occasion—often in fact—bite the hand that feeds me.

Far from being an indictment of the uncouthness of the proletariat, this book focuses on aesthetics that are applicable to the tastes of all classes, indeed, that are very much a part of my own life, from my Sierra Club calendars featuring spectacular vistas of rugged canyons and bald, sunlit buttes to my faux Queen Ann La-z-boy upholstered in a dramatic shade of bordello red, from the irreligious cards I send to my friends at Christmas to the atrocious meals I prepare with crushed potato chips and cans of Campbell's soup. No one is entirely immune to the often irresistible appeal of the tastes I describe, least of all myself. We all eat processed foods and are therefore all at the mercy of the rhetoric of deliciousness; we all pay homage to quaintness with our "distressed" furniture and our collections of Depression glass; we all love to dandle babies and kiss cute puppy dogs; even the very wealthy are obsessed with coolness and the chic of poverty; both middle-class teenagers and Fortune 500 CEOs are fascinated with futuristic war games; and the blight of glamorousness is as prevalent among those who have the means to shop at Barney's as among those who wish that they did.

Moreover, while many critics insist that consumerism is materialistic and jeopardizes our moral welfare, seducing us with the pleasures of the senses and compromising the life of the mind, my own objection is precisely the opposite, that consumerism is not materialistic enough and its aesthetics, far from being shamelessly carnal and sybaritic, remain surprisingly unsensual even as they intoxicate us with their sumptuousness, with the Technicolor light shows of cyberspace and the bravura realism of Hollywood special effects. The uncontained commercial hedonism of the present, had it fulfilled its initial promise, would have represented the culmination of Enlightenment secularism, of the belief in pleasure, in maximizing happiness, in the necessity of enjoying the physical world and using reason to better our lots here on Earth rather than wiling away our time in thankless abstinence in hopes of reaping our just rewards in heaven. Rooted in the senses, in tangible pleasures, consumerism would have been pagan and atheistic. Its god would have been the body. If it had had a concept of the afterlife, it would have been nothing more celestial than a comfortable retirement in a temperate climate.

And yet despite the splendid colors of its Ben Day dots and the gorgeous imagery of its films, consumerism is as symbolic and indifferent to the body as the most traditional forms of religion, and its vision of a material paradise is as inaccessible as the Christian vision of Kingdom Come, an otherworldly mirage that appeals to the imagination, not the senses. Whereas the word "aesthetics" implies a playful degree of libertinism and sensuality, the aesthetics of consumerism are ascetic and cerebral, incorporeal illusions designed to stir up dissatisfaction, to provoke restless longings that cannot be fulfilled. They actively instill anxiety and discontentment with our lot, reinforcing the conviction that others are living lives happier and more interesting than our own, as in the case of fashion magazines, which present mythically beautiful "glamazons" whose willowy perfection has sent many teenagers into a bulemic tailspin; or in the case of cleanness, whose conventions of sparkling lustrousness set impossibly high standards of sanitation for housewives, who fight heroically against slimy green soap scum and ring-around-the-tub. Epicureanism in its historical sense emphasized sufficiency and moderation, preaching autonomy from one's possessions, but consumerist epicureanism emphasizes *in*sufficiency and *im*moderation, preaching slavish dependence on possessions that we cannot afford but that are portrayed as the very prerequisites of happiness.

Anti-consumerist diatribes also single out corporations as the source of all that is crude, manipulative, and mercenary in our society, while they whitewash the consumer as a helpless victim roped to the railroad tracks, mercilessly exploited by money-grubbing financiers who plot our subjugation from the board-rooms of glass towers. Although I myself find it difficult to avoid assigning blame in the chapters that follow and constantly search for the culprit, the villain of the melodrama, reducing an essentially bipartisan rela-tionship to a familiar narrative, the truth, of course, is far more complex. If there *is* a conspiracy, we ourselves are its tacticians, as well as its beneficiaries. The aes-thetics of consumerism are not foisted upon us; they emerge out of a rich and imaginative collaboration be-tween the forces of capitalism and our own fears and desires. If there is kitsch in our daily lives, it is because there is kitsch in our minds. It is we who are to blame, not Madison Avenue. The advertiser has simply taken up residence in the well-appointed quarters we have so obligingly prepared for him in our collective aesthetic unconscious. The stylistic distortions of the market-place often reflect tensions in our attitudes towards the things and people around us: towards our children, whose waywardness we seek to smother beneath the conventions of cuteness; towards parents, whose denial of adolescents' sexuality and independence our off-spring throw back in our faces by adopting the exag-gerated mannerisms of coolness; and even towards computer software, whose gaudy aesthetic emerges from the anarchic aspirations of programmers who seek to hide from themselves the dull, bureaucratic realities of their lives.

The public's nostalgia provides one of the most fertile grounds for advertising. In the ornamental details that lurk in our peripheral vision, it is possible to perceive the anxieties and daydreams of a society still undergoing momentous changes from an agricultural to an industrial economy. One of the primary functions of the aesthetics of consumerism is to provide us with an emotional cushion, a form of camouflage, a credible disguise for a culture that refuses to admit the truth about itself, that self-righteously insists on its own anti-consumerism even while enjoying the luxuries and conveniences of mass production. We continue to pretend that our values are those of Mayberry, an intimate, small-town world full of Mom-and-Pop businesses, rather than an overpopulated megalopolis dominated by multinational cartels. Perhaps the best way to define the word "aesthetics" in application to the artifacts of popular culture is this: They comprise the various masks that hide the true nature of store-bought goods, the wigs and Groucho Marx noses that restore the "aura" of the handmade to our commodities and combat our estrangement from a world packaged in plastic, transforming even computers into a sort of bionic folk art. The aesthetics of consumerism are full of nostalgia, of calculated self-avoidance. They are the rhetorical dodges by which manufacturers purify themselves and overcome their markets' resistance to a highly commercialized society. Not only are assembly-line products described as "handcrafted" and "old-fashioned," but shoppers themselves masquerade in any number of outlandish costumes: as artists in their own right, as committed seekers of self-expression, as snide and skeptical rebels, as disaffected department-store dropouts who haunt flea markets and funky boutiques in search of vintage clothing, and as freelance archeologists bent on preserving the material culture of the past, from rooster weather vanes to hand-cranked coffee grinders.

The aesthetics of consumerism also shore up the consumer's sense of selfhood and individuality, which have been deeply compromised by the conditions of urban society. In a world sensitized to the distastefulness of selling, one in which even the most gullible people recognize how commercial our culture has become, manufacturers have learned to incorporate this distrust into their marketing techniques. They have built into consumerism symbolic forms of resistance to it, ineffectual strategies of rebellion that flatter the consumer with the belief that, far from being a marketing guinea pig, at the mercy of Madison Avenue, he is a courageous loner, a wacky oddball immune to the indoctrination of advertising. One of the key concepts of popular culture is controlled nonconformity: the innocuous methods by which consumers release their frustrations through displays of self-infantilism, whether it be by driving fast cars; buying outrageous outfits; wearing ripped clothing; playing loud music; or wooing their lovers with endearingly nutty courtship rituals that reassure them that, in contrast to corporate drones, they are wild and crazy iconoclasts who "dare to be different." Consumerism has created the perfect disguise for conformity: rebelliousness. Our individuality is actually contingent on our obedience, on buying the same products that millions of other people are buying at exactly the same time in exactly the same stores, all the while laboring under the extraordinary misconception that shopping is a profoundly self-creative act that distinguishes us from the mindless herd.

CUTENESS

S he stands in maroon bloomers and a pink dress that flares tantalizingly above two acrylic legs that descend, unvaried in diameter, all the way down to her gout-stricken ankles crammed into booties. Her feet, crippled and pigeon-toed, touch at their tips. A sassy tuft of a synthetic top-knot sprays out of a helmet of auburn hair encircled by a polka dot bow that sits atop her head like a windmill, dwarfing the rest of her figure. Her nose is no bigger than a button, and her astonishingly candid eyes are two moist pools framed by eyebrows penciled like quizzical circumflexes on the vast dome of her forehead. Emptied of all internal life, these mesmerizing orbs, composing at least 25 percent of a face as wide as her shoulders, stare out directly at us with a reticence heightened by the hec-

1

tic flush of her complexion. Her name is "So Shy
Sherri," and she is one of toy manufacturer Galoob's
nine new "Baby Faces," a set of "super posin'" dolls with
names like "So Sweet Sandi," "So Sorry Sarah," and "So
Delightful Dee Dee," each with an "adorable" expression
and personality of her own.

Everywhere we turn we see cuteness, from cherubic
figures batting their peepers on Charmin toilet paper
to teddy bears frozen mid-embrace, the stubs of their
pawless arms groping for hugs. In the eyes of most people, whose conditioned responses to this most rigid of
styles prevent them from recognizing its artificiality,
things like calendars with droopy-eyed puppies plead-
ing for attention or greeting cards with kitty cats in
raincoats are the very embodiment of innocence and
as such represent an absence of the designed and ma-
nipulated qualities of what is in fact a heavily man-
nered aesthetic. For them, the foreshortened limbs
and sad, saucer eyes of a doll like So Shy Sherri are part
of a unique and readily identifiable iconography whose
distortions trigger, with Pavlovian predictability, maternal feelings for a mythical condition of endearing
naivete. The chilling paradox of the fetishes over which
we croon so irrepressibly is that their cuteness suggests

guilelessness, simplicity, and a refreshing lack of affectation, the very antithesis of what we would expect if we were to judge these toys on the basis of their extreme stylization alone.

Cuteness is not an aesthetic in the ordinary sense of the word and must by no means be mistaken for the physically appealing, the attractive. In fact, it is closely linked to the grotesque, the malformed. So Shy Sherri, for instance, is an anatomical disaster. Her legs are painfully swollen, her fingers useless pink stumps that seem to have been lopped off at the knuckles, and her rosy cheeks so bloated that her face is actually wider than it is long. Medieval or renaissance images of the Christ child, those obese monstrosities whose muscularity always strikes the modern viewer as bafflingly inaccurate, make an interesting comparison. In an era like our own, which prides itself on its ability to achieve effects of uncanny realism, the disfigured putti of the "Baby Face" series of dolls mark a decline rather than an advance in the representation of children, an eerie throwback to the slant-eyed sphinxes in Sienese icons: alien, carnivorous-looking creatures who are, in many ways, as pictorially inexact as So Shy Sherri.

Far from being an accident of bad craftsmanship, the element of the grotesque in cuteness is perfectly deliberate and must be viewed as the explicit intention of objects that elicit from us the complex emotions we feel when we encounter the fat faces and squat, ruddy bodies of creatures like the Trolls, with their pot bellies, pug noses, and teased-up mops of brightly colored hair. The grotesque is cute because the grotesque is pitiable, and pity is the primary emotion of this seductive and manipulative aesthetic that arouses our sympathies by creating anatomical pariahs, like the Cabbage Patch Dolls or even E.T., whose odd proportions and lack of symmetry diverge wildly from the relative balance and uniformity of ordinary bodies. The aesthetic of cuteness creates a class of outcasts and mutations, a ready-made race of lovable inferiors whom both children and adults collect, patronize, and enslave in the protective concubinage of vast harems of homely dolls and snugglesome misfits. Something becomes cute not necessarily because of a quality it has but because of a quality it lacks, a certain neediness and inability to stand alone, as if it were an indigent starveling, lonely and rejected because of a hideousness we find more touching than unsightly.

The koalas, pandas, and lambs of the stuffed animal series "Lost 'n Founds" directly allude to this state of homeless destitution. With their "adorable 'so-sad' eyes" that shed real tears, these shameless examples of the waif or pauper syndrome seem to be begging to be rescued from their defenseless state, so tellingly emphasized by paws as cumbersome as boxing gloves—absurd appendages that lie uselessly in their laps, totally free of any of the prehensile functions hands usually serve. Because it generates enticing images like these of ugliness and dejection, cuteness has become essential to the marketplace, in that advertisers have learned that consumers will "adopt" products that create, often in their packaging alone, an aura of motherlessness, ostracism, and melancholy, the silent desperation of the lost puppy dog clamoring to be befriended—namely, to be bought.

Cuteness, in short, is not something we find in our children but something we *do* to them. Because it aestheticizes unhappiness, helplessness, and deformity, it almost always involves an act of sadism on the part of its creator, who makes an unconscious attempt to maim, hobble, and embarrass the thing he seeks to idolize, as in the case of "Little Mutt," a teddy bear with a game leg that a British manufacturer has even fitted with an orthopedic boot. The process of conveying cuteness to the viewer disempowers its objects, forcing them into ridiculous situations and making them appear more ignorant and vulnerable than they really are. Adorable things are often most adorable in the middle of a pratfall or a blunder: Winnie the Pooh, with his snout stuck in the hive; the 101 dalmatians of Disney's classic, collapsing in double splits and sprawling across the ice; Love-a-Lot Bear, in the movie *The Care Bears*, who stares disconsolately out at us with a paint bucket overturned on his head; or, the grimmest example of the cruelty of cuteness, the real fainting goat, which has acquired of late a perverse chic as a pet (bred with myatonia, a genetic heart defect, it coyly folds up and faints every time you scream at it). Although the gaze we turn on the cute thing seems maternal and solicitous, it is in actuality transformative and will stop at nothing to appease its hunger for expressing pity and big-heartedness, even at the cost of mutilating the object of its affections. The French-manufactured "Vet Set" takes the neediness of cuteness to macabre extremes: The kit is equipped with a wounded stuffed puppy whose imploring eyes seem to wince as it patiently awaits the physician, who can alleviate its suffering with a wide array of bandages, tourniquets, syringes, and even a stethoscope to monitor the irregular, fluttering thump of a mechanical heart that actually beats.

If cuteness is the aesthetic of deformity and dejection, it is also the aesthetic of sleep. Although adorable things can be bright eyed and bushy tailed, the pose we find cutest of all is not that of a rambunctious infant screaming at the top of his lungs but that of the docile sleepyhead, his chin nestled drunkenly in the crook of someone's neck, wearing the pjs in the FAO Schwarz catalog that consist of a full-length leopard suit made of spotted fur or a "sweet confection of lace" with fuzzy marabou touches of pristine white down sewn like a tutu around the waist. The world of cute things is transfixed by the spell of the sandman, full of napping lotus eaters whose chief attraction lies in their dormant and languorous postures, their defenseless immobility.

Turning its targets into statues and plush dolls, cuteness is ultimately dehumanizing, paralyzing its victims into comatose or semi-conscious things. In fact, the "thingness" of cute things is fixed firmly in our minds by means of the exaggerated textures and hues so characteristic of stuffed animals, with their shimmering satins and their luscious coats of fur, or dolls with their luxuriant profusion of hair, often of absurd length and body (as with the Cutie Kids of the "Cutie Club" series, a set of dolls whose psychedelic coiffures cascade down their sides in corkscrew curls longer than their own bodies). "Anxiously awaiting power snuggles," FAO Schwarz's huge grizzly bear is a slouching, seemingly invertebrate mammoth rippling with "serious spreads of soft spots" that are "just asking to be hauled and mauled," while their elephant, as large as a St. Bernard, is described as "big, plump, and deliciously soft with soulful brown eyes that encourage big-time hugging and smooching." Vacant and malleable, animals like these inhabit a world of soothing tactile immediacy in which there are no sharp corners or abrasive materials but in which everything has been conveniently soft-sculpturized to yield to our importunate squeezes and hugs. If such soulless insentience is any indication, cuteness is the most scrutable and externalized of aesthetics in that it creates a world of stationary objects and tempting exteriors that deliver themselves up to us, putting themselves at our disposal and allowing themselves to be apprehended entirely through the senses. In light of the intense physicality of our response to their helpless torpor, our compulsive gropings even constitute something one might call cute sex or, in point of fact, given that one of the partners lies there groggy and catatonic, a kind of necrophilia, a neutered coupling consummated in our smothering embrace of a serenely motionless object incapable of reciprocating. Far from being content with the helplessness of our young as we find them in their natural state, we take all kinds of artificial measures to dramatize this vulnerability even further by defacing them, embarrassing them, devitalizing them, depriving them of their selfhood, and converting them, with the help of all of the visual and sartorial tricks at our disposal, into disempowered objects, furry love balls quivering in soft fabrics as they lapse into withdrawal for their daily fix of TLC.

During the course of the twentieth century, the overwhelming urge to engage in cute sex profoundly affected the appearance of the teddy bear, whom toy manufacturers put on a rich diet, creating an irresistibly moon-faced dough boy whose corpulence invites caressing. The original designs for the teddy bear, produced during the 1880s, were modeled on actual taxidermic specimens and were relatively naturalistic in appearance, disfigured by scholiastic humps that jutted out of their backs, long, vulpine snouts, and slender, simian arms that hung all the way down to their feet. Over the last few decades, Pooh and Paddington have improved their posture, sprouted fat, dwarfish arms, and, moreover, submitted to a barrage of rhinoplastic amputations that has turned their crunching mandibles into harmless bulges that protrude only slightly from round, unthreatening faces. Casting melting glances from sad button eyes, today's winsome "critters" have also been redesigned as more serviceable cute sex toys, much like the gaping-mouthed dolls available in adult book stores: Their arms are now permanently sewn in an outstretched position, rather than dangling at their sides as they once did, simulating an embrace as lifeless as the latex clasp of our "fantasy playmates."

The strange consequence of the need to increase huggability is that all stuffed animals, from marsupials to pachyderms, are covered in fur, regardless of the fact that the real-life counterparts of Beatrice the Boa and Willy the Walrus have scales that are wet and slimy or hides that are bristly and tough. Behind the pleasure we take in the bodies of such cartoon heroes as Kermit and Snoopy is the fear of another sort of body altogether, the distasteful subtext of our plush toys: The excreting bodies of real live babies which, far from being clean and dry, are squalling factories of drool and snot. Our unenviable role as the hygienic custodians of children, whose dirty bottoms we must regularly wipe, noses we must blow, and soiled underwear we must launder, has led to a recurrent parental fantasy, that of the diaperless baby, the excretionless teddy bear, a low-maintenance infant whom we can kiss and fondle free of anxiety that it will throw up on our shoulder as we rock it to sleep or pee in our laps as we dandle it on our knees.

Exaggerating the vast discrepancies of power between the sturdy adult and the enfeebled and susceptible child, the narcissism of cuteness is evident in the way that the aesthetic ascribes human attributes to non-human things. Anthropomorphism is to a large extent *the* rhetorical strategy of children's books, which often generate their narratives from a kind of animal transvestism in which dogs, cats, bears, and pigs have the clothing and demeanor of human beings. Calendars, another rich source of cuteness, also employ animal transvestism as a major theme: mice as prima ballerinas in toe shoes and tutus, dogs in party hats and sunglasses, or swallow-tailed hamsters in tuxes and cummerbunds rearing up on their hind legs to give each other what appears to be an affectionate peck on the cheek. Even an artist as respected as William Wegman subtly refashions, in the appropriative style of postmodernism, the low-brow aesthetic of cuteness by decking out his lugubrious mastiff, an irresistibly funereal pooch cheerlessly resigned to his fate, in everything from Christian Dior to Calvin Klein jeans. Examples like these reveal that the cute worldview is one of massive human chauvinism, which rewrites the universe according to an iconographic agenda dominated by the pathetic fallacy. Multiplying our image a thousand-fold and reverberating like an echo chamber with the familiar sounds of our own voices, the cute vision of the natural world is a world without nature, one that annihilates "otherness," ruthlessly suppresses the non-human, and allows nothing, including our own children, to be separate and distinct from us.

The imitative nature of cuteness can also be seen in the relation of the aesthetic to precocity. One of the things we find cutest in the behavior of our children is their persistence in mimicking us, not only in such time-honored traditions as dress-up (the anthropomorphic version of which is played out obsessively in children's literature) but in that most basic form of child's play, mothering, whether it be of a doll or of a family pet. The spectacle of toddlers rocking their babies, changing the diapers of the many incontinent toys on the market, placating anxious dolls, or thrashing disobedient teddy bears elicits some of our most gloating and unrestrained responses to cuteness. Nothing delights us more than the strange sight of a one-year-old in a stroller meeting a barely ambulatory two-year-old, who, rather than seeking to establish spontaneous esprit de corps with his peer, breaks rank and gibbers baby talk at the bewildered object of his curiously perfunctory affections. As co-conspirators in this game of make-believe maturity, we reward children who at once feign helplessness and assume adult authority in mothering others, reinforcing simultaneously both infantilism and precocity. The child is thus taught not only to be cute in himself but to recognize and enjoy cuteness in others, to play the dual roles of actor and audience, cootchy-cooing as much as he is cootchy-cooed. In this way, our culture actively inculcates the aesthetic doctrines of cuteness by giving our children what amounts to a thorough education in the subject, involving extensive and rigorous training in role-playing. By encouraging our children to imitate the way we ourselves fawn over their own preciousness, we give them the opportunity to know cuteness from both sides of the equation, not only from the standpoint of the object receiving the attention but from the standpoint of those giving it as well, from their appreciative audience-cum-artistic directors, whom they impersonate for brief and touching intervals in their own highly informative charades of child-rearing. We teach our children the nature and value of cuteness almost from the dawn of consciousness and initiate them into the esoteric rituals of its art, passing on to them the tribal legacy of its iconographic traditions, its strange, self-mutilating ceremonies, as alien in their way, at least to a culture unindoctrinated in cuteness, as the scarification customs of Africa or New Guinea. Because imitation allows children to observe their own behavior with the analytic detachment with which they in turn are observed by their admirers, cuteness is unique among aesthetics because it lays the foundations for its own survival by building into itself a form of proselytizing.

The association of cuteness with a delusional state of artlessness prevents us from realizing that the qualities of primitivism and droll savagery around which we have woven this all-consuming folk religion embody something we would *like* to see in children rather than something we actually do see there. The conventions of cuteness are the residue of unfulfilled wishes that crystallize in the gap between the daily realities of children and our quixotic and unobtainable notions of what they should, ideally, be like. Cuteness is every parent's portable utopia, the rose-colored lenses that color and blur the profound drudgery of child-rearing with soft-focused sentimentality. We use it to allay fears of our failures as parents and to numb us to the irritations of the vigilance we must maintain over creatures who are, despite the anesthetizing ideology of cuteness, often more in control of us than we are of them.

Although it is easy to sympathize with the disquieting frustrations that underlie this aesthetic, cuteness is in fact ultimately more a source of unhappiness than of comfort among parents. To superimpose the vast edifice of fetishized images and intricate rituals onto the shallow foundations of a reality that cannot withstand its weight is to invite disappointment, not only for us but for our children. Cuteness saturates the visual landscape of consumerism with utopian images that cause feelings of inadequacy among parents, who inevitably measure the rowdy and selfish behavior of their own children by exacting ideals of tractability, cuddliness, and quiescence. Just as the inundation of our culture with the glitzy images of recent video pornography has elevated our aesthetic standards in regard to our partners (and consequently interfered with our sexual enjoyment of ordinary bodies in all of their imperfections), so cuteness elevates our expectations in regard to our children. It prevents us from enjoying them in their natural, unindoctrinated state, oppressed as we are by our apparent failures as caregivers who strive unavailingly to discern in our headstrong offspring the lineaments of the model child.

The result of this psychological malaise is an entirely new aesthetic, an invention of the last few decades: the anti-cute. In an effort to counteract prevailing images of children, a culture like our own naturally produces as an antidote images of the exact opposite of cuteness: the perverse. Our belief that our children are harmless little cherubs who toss wreathes of posies hither and yon collides with their intransigence and generates in the process so much hostility that we are inclined to view them as corrupt, possessed, even satanic.

Cuteness thus coexists in a dynamic relation with the perverse. The failure of the hyperboles of one aesthetic gives rise to the hyperboles of the other, of the child as the vehicle of diabolical powers from the Great Beyond, which have appropriated the tiny, disobedient bodies of our elfish changelings as instruments for their assaults on the stability of family life. The spate of films about demonic possession shows just how assiduous we have become about building up the new iconography of the anti-cute. Catering to a deep need in the popular imagination, Hollywood has begun to manufacture images that function as outrageous travesties of cuteness, like those found in *Poltergeist*, in which a young girl becomes the conduit of tormented spirits of the damned who emerge from the throbbing blue light of the television set; or in *Child's Play*, in which the spirit of a dead serial killer inhabits the body of a doll named Chuckie, who, stalking down hallways with butcher knives tucked behind its back, murders Aunt Maggie, the baby-sitter, by giving her such a jolt that she staggers backwards out of the kitchen window and plummets ten floors to splatter on the hood of a parked car. Similarly, in David Cronenberg's *The Brood*, the protagonist's children, a pack of dwarfish gnomes, gestate in moldy embryonic sacks hanging outside of her belly and then, after birth, begin spontaneously to respond to her volatile moods, ultimately bludgeoning her mother to death with kitchen utensils in a fit of rage.

Although it is still the dominant mode of representing children, cuteness is an aesthetic under siege, the object of contempt, laughter, and skepticism. Its commercialized aura of greeting card naivete makes it so fragile, so vulnerable to ridicule, that it cannot withstand the frank realism with which matters of parenting, divorce, and sexuality are now being addressed by the public at large. In the last few decades, cuteness has been subjected to remorseless satire as we attempt to loosen the grip of its iconography on an imagination hungry for images closer to the harsh realities of the era of the latchkey kid, the two-career family, the single-parent household, the crack baby, and the less-than-innocent, drug-running sixth-grader with a beeper in one pocket and a .44 Magnum automatic pistol in the other. Loud and chaotic, *The Simpsons* is the anti-cute show of the 1990s, the "all-American dysfunctional family," as they have been nicknamed. Their household constitutes a direct subversion of the insipidity of cuteness, with its cartoon characters' harshly contoured shapes, gaping, lipless mouths, and enormous boiled-egg eyes goggling in such a way as to suggest the mindless somnambulism of compulsive TV viewers. The anti-cute launches a frontal assault on fuzzy-wuzziness with a blitz of images of the child as the petulant and demanding brat who disdains the sacrosanct laws of property ownership, gleefully annihilating cuisinarts and microwaves as he mows a broad swathe of destruction through the household's inner sanctum.

With the rise of the anti-cute, we are witnessing what amounts to civil war in the contemporary aesthetic of the family, a battle in which the image of the child as the unnatural spawn of Satan, an impish spirit of pure malevolent mischievousness, has locked horns with that of the child as the inanimate stuffed animal. Generating their plots by pitting the cute against the anti-cute, Parts 1 and 2 of *Gremlins* provide a kind of allegory of this transformation. In Part 2, the adorable "Gizmo" (an appropriate name for this standard-bearer of cuteness, because it emphasizes the animal's status as an inert object) purrs with a contented coo, its droopy ears and sad eyes inviting the lubricious embraces of cute sex. After it is exposed to water, however, it begins to reproduce, laying eggs that enter a larval stage in repulsive cocoons covered by viscous membranes. Whereas Gizmo is soft, dry, and relatively well behaved, the ferocious aliens that quickly hatch from their water-induced hibernation are, as one character calls them, "ugly, slimy, mean-spirited, and gloppy." In them, both the behavior and appearance of cute objects are at once evoked and subverted. Gizmo's strokeable fur is transformed into a wet, scaly integument, while the vacant portholes of its eyes (the most important facial feature of the cute thing, giving us free access to its soul and ensuring its total scrutability, its incapacity to hold back anything) become diabolical slits hiding a lurking intelligence, just as its dainty paws metamorphose into talons and its pretty puckered lips into enormous Cheshire grimaces with full sets of sharp incisors. Whereas cute things have clean, sensuous surfaces that remain intact and unpenetrated (suggesting, in fact, that there is nothing at all inside, that what you see is what you get), the anti-cute Gremlins are constantly being squished and disemboweled, their entrails spilling out into the open, as they explode in microwaves and are run through paper shredders and blenders. With the help of food and water, they multiply exponentially and begin their devastating campaign—Hollywood's favorite plot device—against property ownership, destroying in Part 1 an entire town and, in Part 2, a skyscraper modeled on the Trump Tower. In this Manichean contrast between the precious Gizmo and its progeny, the hyperactive vandals who incarnate a new but equally stylized representation of youth and innocence, *Gremlins* neatly encapsulates the iconographic challenges to an aesthetic that is gradually relinquishing its hold on the popular imagination as we attempt to purge ourselves of the antiquated religion of infantilism.

QUAINTNESS

A t the raucous blow-outs of the Society for Creative Anachronism, members from the far-flung corners of the "Knowne Worlde," from Poughkeepsie to Tuscaloosa, immerse themselves in the "mythos" of the Middle Ages by engaging in a wide variety of "medieval party type activities," including tavern brawls in which lecherous churls abduct buxom bar "wenches" and jousting matches in which knights in full armor stage "Whack-a-Roo Tourneys," clobbering each other with fiberglass javelins and "siege rocks" made of tennis balls wrapped in duct tape. Formed during the 1960s by a group of sci-fi aficionados (who just happen to "like being medieval so they can relax and have a good time"), the SCA comprises, by its own reckoning, a disproportionate number of computer jocks who seek to know "the emotional reality of former times," not through litanies of facts, but through reenactments that involve "step[ping] through a time warp" and adopting the names and personalities of such people as the Countess Elspeth of Stonehaven or Oisin Dubh mac Lochlainn. The group adheres so scrupulously to the philosophy that "ambience is everything" that they dress themselves for their events by buying greaves and visors at Ye Olde Kutting Edge Armory, which offers "quality, affordable armour" "for the discriminating SCA fighter," and Howdy Garb, which advertises—with Madison Avenue flair—a distinguished line of machine-washable tunics and cod pieces: "a jerkin *makes* a 'Renaissance man'. . . . Try them with tights, pants or a kilt for the look that's perfect for you!"

What the SCA calls the "living history movement" reduces the past to a sword-and-sorcery mise-en-scène straight out of a Universal Studios theme park, an imaginary kingdom in which inebriated ruffians engage in "wassail-making," holding beer chugging contests with tankards brimming with mead. If historians seek to know the past intellectually, those who revel in that most ahistorical of aesthetics, quaintness, seek to know it sensually, not through knowledge but through atmosphere, stripping it of facts and mining it for sensations. Quaintness focuses squarely on the physicality of Olden Times, on their creature comforts, and is therefore set more often in the nineteenth century than the Middle Ages, which bring to mind cold flagstone floors and drafty, smoke-filled dining halls draped in mildewed tapestries, whereas the nineteenth century conjures up images of toasty Christmas interiors, brisk sleigh rides, and cups of piping hot cocoa. Quaintness reproduces the past selectively, editing out its discomfort, inconvenience, misery, stench, and filth and concentrating instead on its carnal pleasures, its "warm and homey feelings." The people who lived in "the rustic idyll" were always "snug as bugs in a rug," to quote Laura Ingalls Wilder's novel *Little House on the Prairie*, a manifesto of quaintness that portrays the ascetic life of the homesteader as an almost sybaritic existence spent around the hearth, lulled by the dulcet strains of "Pa" playing "Highland Mary" on the fiddle. Although technological advances have made contemporary life infinitely more comfortable than the past, we persist in believing that the days of yore were much cozier than the present, which, if it is to be endured at all, must be recreated in the image of the log cabin, where ladies in gingham granny dresses baked gingerbread cookies in potbellied stoves.

In keeping with an aesthetic that simultaneously sensualizes and de-intellectualizes history, quaintness is intimately bound up with all aspects of food preparation, which have undergone such radical changes within the last 100 years that our duties in the kitchen have been reduced to zapping pouches in the microwave and pureeing protein frappes in the Cuisinart. The aesthetic is often a meditation on the evolution of kitchen appliances and the enormous strides we have made in simplifying the unpleasantness of housework, whose backbreaking horrors we evoke by displaying around our rooms spinning jennies and hand-cranked egg beaters, "quirky and unlabor-saving genuine articles" that were once operated by the brute force of hyperventilating housewives. The quaintness of a butter churn or a wringer washing machine often derives, not from its ingeniousness, but from how much time it wasted, from its inefficiency, and from the touchingly absurd indefatigability of its users, those indentured kitchen slaves who thrashed rugs permeated with the soot of fossil fuels and milked the family cow at the crack of dawn. In an era of self-defrosting freezers, microwave espresso machines, In-Sink-Erators, and self-cleaning cat litter boxes with laser-beam eyes, labor itself has become quaint and the conspicuous consumption of time has been aestheticized, transformed into a prurient spectacle for a generation that, accustomed to the luxuries of mechanization, reenacts the past as a form of recreation, performing such activities as crocheting afghans, making candles, and baking cakes from scratch.

Although our admiration of old-fashioned things would seem to celebrate the industriousness of those who lived without the benefit of CoffeeMate coffee makers and "Whisper Quiet" dishwashers, as well as the inventors of such contraptions as hand-cranked wall phones, monocycles, and cistern toilets, quaintness is in fact a patronizing aesthetic. It ridicules the technological red herrings of the past and exalts the superior ingenuity of the present, with its "Light Therapy Illuminators" that alleviate SAD (Seasonal Affective Disorder) and its "germicidal warm-mist humidifiers" whose "ultra violet light chambers" destroy Staph bacteria and E. coli. The supercilious scrutiny of our culture's industrial infancy can be compared to the way in which children observe ants tunneling through the soil of glass terrariums as they laboriously move bread crumbs through subterranean chambers, a Herculean feat that the child watches with feelings of exhilarating omnipotence, fully aware that he or she could perform the task effortlessly. Quaintness pretends to be an aesthetic that brings alive the reality of the hardscrabble days when pioneers in covered wagons dodged flaming arrows and mountaineers in coon caps drank scalding swigs of white lightning, but in fact it is one of the primary aesthetics of modernity. Fixated on the present, it flatters our own cunning at the expense of the ineffectuality of a period whose ignorance we exploit as a foil to the wizardry of modern gadgets.

The disrespect for the past implicit in quaintness also emerges in the burgeoning collectibles movement, whose followers comb through the debris of garage sales and "Rummage Shoppes" in search of copper bed warmers and antique beer steins. We are so estranged from the past that we turn old utensils into the exact opposite of utensils, into objets d'art, modernist sculptures denuded of both meaning and utility, as in the case of the collector who mounted on a pedestal in his living room an ancient Waterwitch outboard boat motor manufactured by Sears, Roebuck, a battered hulk of aluminum and steel whose subtle curves bring to mind the works of Brancusi and Arp. Just as the Western world imperialistically absconds with the masks of Africa and displays them to fashionable urbanites in Soho galleries, so quaintness imperialistically ransacks the kitchens, general stores, and tool sheds of the past for the rusty spoils of old Bissel carpet sweepers, National cash registers, and Corona manual typewriters, which are displayed as gigantic tchotchkes, apt symbols of how we have ceased to understand and interact with history, which has become nothing more than a cornucopia of bright ideas for women's magazines. We tell ourselves that, by appreciating quaintness, we are getting closer to the past and demonstrating our reverence for the quality of its craftsmanship, but in fact our cult of bygone days reveals that we hold our forebears and their inventions in contempt and that history has receded altogether from our lives, leaving behind the wreckage of archaic appliances, which we have salvaged from the shores of time and converted into ornaments for our kitchens and living rooms.

While homeowners wax lyrical over clawfoot bathtubs and the merchandise available at Renovation Hardware, they are often deeply ashamed of their own appliances, which are exiled into cupboards, banished into closets, and locked away in drawers, with ugly modern sinks hidden by gathered cloth skirts, toilet brushes by ceramic ewers, and radiators by clever paint jobs that "sponge them into invisibility." The followers of quaintness both admire the cumbersome rotary flower sifters and mechanical tin juicers of the past and abhor their own utensils, the "unlovely equipment and cleaning supplies" which must be "kept out of sight [so that] you have room to make the most of [the antique collectibles] you want to have on view." Quaintness creates two houses: the ancient one on display, a rustic festival of stoneware crock pots and cast-iron cherry stoners, and the modern one barricaded behind a wall of archaic bric-a-brac, which conceals all traces of the distasteful present and thus creates an architecturally schizophrenic space full of consumerist shame about labor.

Quaintness is an aesthetic of clutter, of manic busyness, of exposed beams crowded with hammered brass wall plaques depicting handsome lovers trysting with innocent young maidens, and specially designed "art walls" jam-packed with rooster weather vanes purchased at such stores as Thee Amish Shoppe, Junk-A-

Tique, and The Whatnot Barn. Quaintness is an aesthetic of "stuff," as in the article "Show Your Stuff" in
the magazine *Country Decorating Ideas* ("If you've got it,
here are a half-dozen ways to flaunt it"), or in the profile in *Country Decorator* entitled "Cheerful Clutter," a
photographic essay about two Oregonian pack rats
who, in the course of a lifetime of collecting, have
amassed over "28,000 pounds of 'stuff'," from harmon-
icas and music boxes to framed mottoes and carved
walking sticks. Having moved, at great expense, over
twenty-one times in a little over thirty-six years, from
Alaska to Germany, they have attempted to make "their
many temporary homes as warm . . . as possible" by
scrupulously adhering to a simple decorating credo:
"When you think you've run out of room, stack!" This
philosophy of housekeeping has produced a "country
cottage" that resembles a jumbled attic full of disorga-
nized "treasures" strewn about so carelessly that it is difficult to imagine anyone living in their midst without
tripping over the banjos propped up against the pipe
organ or the porcelain dolls sitting astride the roughhewn rocking horses. At the heart of quaintness is the
baroque—indeed, the rococo. The belief that "more is
more" is the basic axiom of an aesthetic that frantically

31

attempts to leave "not an inch of wasted space" and to create the ostensibly charming impression of a rat's nest, a disheveled look best understood as a frontal assault on modernist austerity, on the antiseptic emptiness of Le Corbusier's white cube. Full of contempt for the industrial idiom of the avant garde, quaintness represents the rage of the middle brow against brainy minimalist elegance, against fashionably barren rooms that, far from projecting that "lived-in feel," emanate an alienating sterility.

Ironically, however, while quaintness rebels against the cerebral meagerness of the Bauhaus school, its own lavishness expresses perfectly the essence of modernity. The unconvincing facsimiles in women's magazines of nineteenth-century living rooms piled to the rafters with a profusion of "stuff" are not literal representations of how old rooms would have looked, since the middle class once owned far fewer things, but are the outcome of viewing the past through the lens of conspicuous consumption, through impulse shopping, so that history looks far more plentiful and abundant than it would have during its day. Imposing a vision of history based on excess on the relatively spare rooms of the past represents a perversion of antiquated forms of interior decoration, which, with the exception of opulent Victorian follies, were not warehouses spilling over with a superabundance of possessions, meccas of accessories modeled on the aisles of Macy's and Nieman Marcus.

In a consumerist society, collecting serves a very specific psychological function. While roaming around the countryside, hunting for bargains, the gourmand of garbage gives a clever spin to the act of shopping. He recharacterizes his materialism as an activity of a higher magnitude, not a selfish act of purchasing a product but a custodial one of salvaging the past, the conscientious work of a dedicated folk archeologist who excavates forgotten windfalls that might otherwise have ended up, with potentially disastrous consequences, in careless hands. Collecting is part of a dialogue that the consumer is having with his own conscience, a way of venting remorse for his acquisitiveness by reconfiguring his spending sprees as the freelance scholarship of a disinterested pseudo-scientist who performs a selfless civic duty of curating and conserving the material culture of the past.

Quaintness is also an aesthetic of clutter because it presents different periods simultaneously. Its chaotic style, reminiscent of many chain restaurants, which cram their dining rooms with old pickle barrels, buggy wheels, and antique German salt pigs, is the outcome of its historical fallaciousness, its scrambled sense of chronology, which mixes together disparate epochs and cultures, collapsing the time line like an accordion. Homeowners rarely have the knowledge, patience, or even interest to recreate a single style of interior decoration, but instead cobble together a generic past, a moody, atmospheric gestalt of what might be called "pastness," a perfectly imaginary representation of the good old days that pays cursory homage to the artifacts of any number of archaic civilizations. Quaintness rides roughshod over authenticity. It avoids verisimilitude and presents a hodgepodge of oldnesses, with ten-gallon cowboy hats displayed on the same shelf with colonial milk pitchers, Deco cake mixers with nineteenth-century pewter mugs, lava lamps with "classic wooden replicas of yesteryear's mantel clocks."

Quaintness is an aesthetic not only of clutter but also of imperfections, of scratches, chips, and cracks. It loathes the regularity of modern products so completely that it goes out of its way to create artificial irregularities in brand new things, thus faking the necessary dilapidation of quaintness, as when decorators "distress" exposed beams with motor oil and drill bits to counterfeit smudges of soot and the ravages of woodworm. Women's magazines frequently offer advice on improvising a "convincing and comforting air of antiquity," of the "authentically rustic," by "worrying" flea market finds "with sandpaper to simulate years of affectionate use," laundering Pendleton blankets fifty times in cold water to create "a little false aging," "mellowing" towels in a weak solution of cold tea, and staining concrete floors with shoe polish to create "authentic-looking discolorations that suggest the passage of time." Just as cuteness sadistically disfigures representations of children to make them pitiable, so quaintness actively disfigures possessions to eradicate the stigma of their newness, their disturbingly characterless perfection, which smacks of the alienating anonymity of assembly lines. These consumerist hate crimes express the discontent of a culture trapped in an eternal present, one in which everything is brand new, squeaky-clean, packaged in Styrofoam peanuts and shrink-wrapped. No sooner do our possessions begin to deteriorate, becoming scuffed and dented, dulled by grime and corroded by rust, than they are summarily discarded for ever-more-advanced models of the same appliances, ever-more-gleaming and untarnished ice crushers and trash compactors. In a consumerist society, signs of obsolescence become a social liability, an indication that one is financially unable to replace the aging product: to ditch the broken-down jalopy, to get rid of the patched blue jeans and the threadbare overcoat, whose shabbiness becomes a conspicuous badge of economic hardship, of the demeaning poverty of the disadvantaged, who must dress themselves and furnish their houses with the dusty white elephants and tattered hand-me-downs of more affluent classes. To ensure that consumers constantly replace their possessions, manufacturers have stigmatized the worn and out-of-date and in the process have produced a world that, out of psychological necessity, purges the environment of objects that betray use, creating a timeless landscape from which all signs of history, of wear and tear, have been eerily eradicated.

The scarification rituals of quaintness offer a way of registering a complaint against the tyranny of the new, an environment that has obtained factitious immortality through the constant replacement of our possessions. And yet the controlled nonconformity of quaintness never really seeks to substitute wood-burning stoves for Westinghouse range tops or old corrugated washboards for new Maytags. Instead, it seeks to preserve the consumerist status quo by restoring to our lives an artificial sense of the passage of time, a token presence of history, which we manufacture by torturing new possessions with heat guns or by acquiring forgeries of anachronistic appliances. Elmira Stove Works, for example, offers self-cleaning black metal ovens and "antique-styled" dishwashers that counteract the laboratory featurelessness of the modern kitchen's white Frigidaires and chrome-and-steel toasters with clunky reproductions of cast-iron warhorses with claw feet and pop-up drawers that conceal the control knobs: "It's like taking a step back in time with Cook's Delight. Stoves that look like 19th century heirlooms but are decidedly new in features and conveniences beyond their historic and inviting facades." Even as we claim to detest the present and portray ourselves as the saboteurs and malcontents of consumerism, committing strategic atrocities against store-bought goods, our rebellion against the tyranny of the new is patently ineffectual.

Descriptions of quaint objects use the words "character" and "charm" to distinguish them from mass-produced products bereft of "aura," as in statements that
assert that "a great deal of the charm of antique furniture lies in the loving care that previous owners have
expended on it," that handmade things retain "strong
dashes of the owner's character," and that "a few nicks
and scratches to the paint add character and a touch of
whimsy" to one's furnishings. Such comments suggest
that quaintness is highly anthropomorphic. It is animistic in its belief that old things absorb the emotions
and personalities of the people who use them, that they
have photographic memories, total recall, so that
creaky Adirondack chairs and saggy four-poster beds
become ghost-ridden mausoleums haunted by family
spirits. From generations of contact with people, old
Hoosier cabinets and massive eighteenth-century sideboards transcend their inanimacy to become eyewit-
nesses of our lives, historians that emanate an almost
occult energy, as if they had stored up the vital forces of
their former proprietors. Behind the superstitious belief that quaint furnishings retain the quirks and habits
of the human beings who rub up against them, tena-
ciously hoarding their passions until they are engorged

with "character," is the equally superstitious belief that modern materials such as plastic, Formica, and stainless steel, with their smooth impermeable surfaces and "aggressively shiny finishes," repel human emotions and therefore never acquire the "friendliness" and "warmth" of quaint "porous" things. Quaintness sets up a dialogue between non-consumerized and consumerized objects, between anti-commodities and commodities, between soulful woods and soullessly inanimate plastics whose pristine surfaces are hermetically sealed against the world, unlike the scratched surfaces of wormy oaks and knotty pines whose chips and cracks function as the orifices of quaintness, the perforations that permit the absorption of their owners' spirit. The primitive belief that our possessions have souls has never disappeared from our culture, and in fact has been reawakened in the twentieth century by consumerism and the tyranny of the new, which have given rise to a new folk religion whose purpose is to restore to our possessions their inner lives. Like many spiritual conversions, this process is often violent, involving mutilation, the forcible opening of the surfaces of an object. One of the reasons old toys are so quaint is that new toys take the de-featuring effects of consumerism to such extremes, with their Day-Glo colors, synthetic materials, rounded edges, and absence of removable parts that might asphyxiate omnivorous children. Items such as corn husk dolls, Raggedy Anns, and hobbyhorses with frazzled manes of yarn are symbolic anti-commodities in contrast to the super-commodities of Mattel and Disney, the sort of dead acrylics eschewed by Ye Olde Toy Shoppe, which invites its customers to "think back . . . back . . . back to the days before the Power Rangers, before Batman and Robin, before Pogs were invented, before Ninja Turtles. . . . back. . . . back . . . to a different memory . . . a different time, a different life!"

In the course of the twentieth century, the duties of the typical housewife have been entirely redefined. An individual who was once a janitor and drudge, her lank hair dripping with sweat as she pummeled bread and cranked clothes through the wringer washer, is suddenly an artiste, an immaculate Martha Stewart who no longer cleans her house so much as she beautifies it, turning tin cans into garden lanterns and covering pillows in linen cases dyed "melon" and "tangerine," thus altering "the flavor of the space completely, the way a squeeze of lemon *transforms* a glass of iced tea." As electrical devices drastically reduced the amount of housework once per-

formed by women in the nineteenth century, the housewife experienced a crisis of identity. She was forced to fill
her increasingly vacant hours by poring over women's
magazines for advice on how to build what has become,
not a simple residence, but a massive, site-specific art in-
stallation project. The quaint, over-decorated look of the
modern house is directly linked to the lack of utility of
its central fixture, the housewife herself, who now seeks
to assuage her growing sense of uselessness by squandering her time on aesthetic rather than practical
chores, on tacking up vintage tea towels as stylish, triangular window valances, dressing the edges of shelves with
feminizing strips of eyelet lace, and upholstering the
seats of chairs with embroidered samplers.

Quaintness also compensates for the absence of real
personal history in our houses. Most dwellings are now
just temporary encampments set up by professional
vagabonds who flee from one residence to the next,
rarely occupying a house for more than seven years before it is thrown onto the market and deserted as too
small, too dark, or too damp. The dynastic legacy of the
old homestead, handed down from one generation to
the next, is largely a thing of the past, a casualty of the
unstable lives of roving yuppies, who are always search-

ing for ever-more-lucrative jobs in ever-more-remote parts of the country, no sooner settling down in the suburbs than they hammer in the for-sale sign. In an age of constant relocations, our houses never acquire the look of permanence that derives from a lifetime of residing in the same rooms that our fathers and mothers lived in, as well as *their* fathers and mothers, who turned their homes into domestic museums, genealogical shrines full of the heirlooms of the entire clan. In a world in which we are cut off in our own temporal vacuum, our own architectural void, in generic, vinyl-sided boxes slapped together from uninviting concretes, plasterboards, and plywoods, we compensate for our sense of uprootedness by creating a sepia-tinted simulacrum of history from do-it-yourself tips in women's magazines, buying heirlooms rather than inheriting them, submerging ourselves in "instant" traditions. Quaintness is consumerism's answer to the extinction of the old homestead, the ancestral hall, which now comes out of a can, complete with moss, ivy, and periodic sightings of the family ghost. The desire to establish continuity with the past is so strong that Disney's CEO Michael Eisner has even built a replica of an archaic small town, Celebration, a real live Lake

Wobegon where housewives gossip over clotheslines and, in the evening, shoot the breeze on "oversized porches and verandahs that encourage old-time neighborhood socializing." With a population of well over 700, this corporate utopia tries to capture "what made communities great in the past" when people stayed put, never straying beyond the borders of the one-horse hamlets in which they were born and raised, plowing the same fields their grandfathers plowed and marrying the farmer's daughter next door.

Just as the house is now cut off from time, so it is cut off from nature. It exists in its own biosphere, in a windless, unnaturally calm twilight zone that we ourselves control by adjusting the dials of our thermostats and central air conditioners, which have made our residences immune to changes in weather, while the invention of electrical lights has liberated them from the cycle of day and night. Quaintness artificially restores to our houses a sense of belonging to their environment rather than being isolated from it, safely contained within their own glass bubbles. It rejects the invulnerability of modern dwellings and evokes a time before fiberglass insulation blocked out icy drafts, before rubberized roofing kept our ceilings from springing leaks, and before exterminators annihilated infestations of disease-carrying vermin. Because quaintness seeks to dramatize the coziness of shelter, it exaggerates both the threat of the elements—howling nor'easters, blinding snow squalls—and the inconvenience of the seasons, which are organized according to a strict aesthetic hierarchy, with winter being quainter than summer and night being quainter than day. Christmas cards, for instance, often consist of Currier & Ives images of warm domestic scenes drawn from the point of view of a shivering peeping Tom whose discomfort, as he gazes enviously through the window, serves as a foil to the untroubled serenity of a touching vignette in which families huddle around roaring fires sipping mulled apple cider while candles twinkle on trees festooned with candy canes. Iconographically, quaintness is extremely voyeuristic and indiscreet, because the windows of snowbound Hallmark-card cabins rarely have curtains, thus offering unobstructed views into rooms whose familial snugness is heightened by the freezing menace of the outside world, an effect that enhances something that the impregnability of the contemporary house makes us take for granted: the luxury of shelter, of a safe haven from the storm.

Quaintness is the aesthetic of chiaroscuro, of smoky paraffin lamps and flickering tapers, of a world of shadows and dark corners in which the fireplace creates an enticingly secure pool of light where people once knitted tea cozies, told tall tales, and played with their children. The absence of diffused electric lighting and central heating in nineteenth-century homes meant that families were forced to gather around stoves and candles, which became the hubs of domestic life, whereas the conveniences of the modern house tend to destroy this spirit of physical togetherness and disperse its occupants, allowing them to wander off to their separate rooms, where they indulge in anti-social activities like listening to their Walkman or playing Nintendo on their computers. Quaintness implicitly comments on the architectural fragmentation of the nuclear family and derives some of its nostalgia from the decline of old-fashioned togetherness, of the close-knit unity fostered by the exigencies of cold and darkness, which prevented sullen teenagers from stalking off to their distant lairs or misanthropic fathers, fugitives from nagging wives and squalling infants, from sequestering themselves in their woodworking shops. Through pictorial images of parents and children peacefully communing before the open hearth, whittling sticks and darning socks, quaintness mourns the loss of cohesion in family life, of the intimate circle brought together by darkness and cold weather.

Quaintness is a democratic aesthetic that abhors luxury and elegance as disturbing symptoms of immodesty and decadence, of self-indulgent showiness, the sickly exhibitionism of the voluptuary who violates "the honest spirit of the country look," its "authenticity." The affluent settings of Hollywood costume dramas, with their Tiffany candelabra, ormolu clocks, Sevres porcelain, Sargent portraits, and Hepplewhite sideboards, are never quaint, because quaintness glorifies the unassuming industriousness of both the lower middle class and the proletariat, who eke out a meager livelihood, eschewing a prosperous "lifestyle" for an abstemious but virtuous existence redolent with American purity and patriotism. The look (if not the reality) of lean times is so seductive to the contemporary housewife that she often hams up the quaintness of her house, mimicking the straitened circumstances of the simple church mouse who, no matter how deep her pockets, pretends to be an honest pauper reduced to high-minded poverty, forced to decorate her rooms on a shoestring. One of the "plots" of quaintness is that of an indigent yet dainty little lady who ingeniously "makes do," cleverly recycling the things at hand, concocting a dining room table out of a barn door set on two sawhorses, a coffee table out of a wobbly cobbler's bench, or even a decorative basket for a house plant out of a floppy old hat. This game of poetic substitution is key to the play-acting, the theater of quaintness, which pits a highly feminine sensibility against a decidedly unfeminine environment: the impoverished village or the inhospitable prairie, over which the housewife eventually triumphs, creating a pocket of civilization in the wilderness. In an effort to convey the illusion of dignity and decorousness maintained in adversity, quaintness often conjoins opposites, delighting in visual paradoxes, placing the ultra-feminine next to the unpolished and the coarse: a pink ribbon tied around a twig chair, a china cup resting on a roughhewn beam, dried flowers spilling out of a rusty camp coffeepot, or vintage lace pantaloons and confirmation dresses tacked up at random on log cabin walls. The seemingly inappropriate juxtaposition of fragile, dainty items and crude, unfinished ones tells the tale of a courageous aesthete living in a state of deprivation, a decorative emergency that requires the imposition of the fierce feminine will on the unmanageable outback, a desolate wasteland that thwarts her aesthetic impulses at every juncture but that is nonetheless ultimately conquered by her creativity, her uncanny knack of making beauty out of nothing. It is perhaps because of this plot that quaintness is so appealing to the contemporary homemaker, who constructs high historical drama from the simple act of interior decoration, traveling back to a time when women were forced to work magic with their scarce resources, assembling dolls out of shriveled gourds and quilts out of worn-out pieces cut from old nightshirts and overcoats.

If cuteness is the aesthetic of childhood, quaintness is the aesthetic of old age. Just as it helps disguise the brand new split-level as an ancient farm house that has been in the family for generations, so it also endows new commodities with a false history, turning them into stolid, tried-and-true staples that have remained immutable throughout the decades, like Quaker Oats and Pure-Castile Peppermint Soap, whose manufacturers self-consciously resist innovations in their products' design. The cover girl of quaint advertising is the grandmother, plump, well-fed, her distinguished grey hair pulled back in a severe bun, whereas the cover girl of a great deal of modern advertising is the bosomy blonde babe who sells it with sleaze, leaning languorously against the door of a luxury Seville or slinking obliviously down the beach as beefy muscle boys hoot and holler. The aura of antiquity provided by the grandmother, the sexually neutral trademark of everything from apple sauce and instant soups to low-fat TV dinners and dietetic salad dressings, helps solve one of the most intractable problems of consumerism: our deep-seated distrust of advertising and our fear of shoddy goods, of being swindled by high-pressure salesmanship. To undercut the rising consumer awareness of the pitfalls of mass production and the chicanery of PR, companies calculatingly reject the seductive gimmicks of modern advertising and plaster their products with stodgy old women whose studied lack of glamor and sex appeal suggests that their product can appeal to the consumer on its own merits, without the help of Madison Avenue. Quaintness in advertising shows consumerism correcting itself, disassociating itself from its own self-aggrandizing techniques, hiding consumerism from the consumer and ostensibly rejecting the commercialism on which it is based. Quaintness alludes to a time *before* consumerism when products were not actively marketed to the public but sold *themselves* on the basis of their reputation for sturdy reliability and not on the basis of their flashy labels and wacky television ads featuring can-can lines of happy cats meowing to snappy jingles and breakfast cereals so fresh that they leap out of their bowls and serenade us like barbershop quartets.

Aesthetics such as quaintness rectify problems that consumerism itself creates and even pretend to loathe its flimsy, mass-produced goods which, if they are to be sold to markets wary of being gouged by both high prices and false promises, must be disguised as one-of-a-kind art objects handcrafted by nimble-fingered grannies in gingerbread cottages, far away from the ominous specter of dark, satanic mills. The corporate purpose of quaintness is to offer consumers symbolic ways of expressing discontent with a mercenary culture and to neutralize the feelings of inferiority caused by constantly buying what they are told to buy. Manufacturers have learned to play upon our contempt for consumerism, to convince us that we are free-spirited rebels and that they themselves, far from being profiteering, multinational cartels, are dusty trading posts on Main Street, a bustling, cobblestone thoroughfare lined with cigar store Indians, picket fences, and apothecary signs.

COOLNESS

A t the end of Godard's *Breathless*, Jean Paul Belmondo is trapped in a police dragnet and shot in the back as he runs down the street, staggering for nearly a block before falling face-first on the pavement, casually puffing a cigarette even as his knees buckle and his eyes begin to glaze over. In the face of death, he remains blasé and imperturbable, exhibiting an unearthly sangfroid that can also be seen in the surly punk in *Rebel Without a Cause* who, during a game of chicken, casually combs his hair, gazing admiringly at his image in the rearview mirror, while he slams the gas pedal to the floor and speeds towards the edge of the cliff. Similarly, the beautiful blonde in Paul Morrisey's *Mixed Blood* continues speaking after she is shot point-blank in the head, turning to her lover, as she slumps in her chair, her hair matted with gore, and apologizing, with implausible presence of mind, "I must look like a mess."

The stylish unflappability of these martyred saints of coolness has a number of cultural antecedents: the brooding virility of the detectives in film noir and hardboiled fiction, the studied hipness of beatniks and jazz musicians, and, perhaps most important, the repressed violence of proletarian youth, of home boys and gangbangers whose phlegmatic, "don't-fuck-with-me" poutiness is more than just a colorful affectation, as insignificant as their Tommy Hilfiger parkas and Nike sweats. Their contemptuous disengagement serves a utilitarian function in an increasingly uncontrollable urban environment, where chaos breeds fantasies of exaggerated self-possession. Coolness is an aesthetic of the streets, a style of deportment specifically designed to alert potential predators that one is impregnable to assault, to prevent skirmishes with lurking thugs ready to waylay nervous cowards who let down their guard and betray their faint-heartedness while scurrying through bombed-out barrios. Far from reflecting confidence, coolness grows out of a sense of threat, of the strain of living in metropolitan war zones where our equanimity is constantly being challenged, giving rise to a hyper-masculine folk religion that fetishizes poise and impassivity. Its often hilarious mannerisms, its swaggering gait and hostile stares, constitute a pragmatic form of aesthetic self-defense, a disguise that fends off aggression through a flamboyant charade of toughness and authority, a truculent insularity that provides psychological camouflage for the ghetto dweller, projecting fearlessness and tranquillity amidst danger.

As one pop culture pundit has so succinctly put it, "where the ghetto goes, the suburbs follow." Attracted by the menacing nonchalance of coolness, prosperous white youth have turned a form of behavior adapted for a very specific social milieu into an aesthetic plaything, mimicking gestures and facial expressions designed as deterrents to attack even in situations in which there is no threat, in which the glowering introversion of the mall rat seems entirely gratuitous, having been removed from its original context, where survival often depends on feigning an air of unruffled calm. The worship of the ghetto has even led the white rapper Vanilla Ice to invent for himself a spurious war record, complete with mendacious scars, the proud stigmata of the five knife fights that this self-styled gang member asserts he only miraculously survived, an un-substantiated claim that has since been refuted by the press, which has revealed that he grew up far from the fray, in a wealthy suburb. Suburban coolness, in short, is mean-street behavior without mean streets, the bed-room community in search of the ghetto, the inner city bused into the burbs for a party on a cul-de-sac, where it has become part of the imposture of privileged youth desperate to rid themselves of what they perceive as the taint of inauthenticity.

The chic of poverty is central to advertising directed at the youth market. The origins of coolness in the in-stability of the inner city can be seen in ads that con-front us with a wall of scowling teenagers in dark shades, their arms folded threateningly over their chests, looking bored and volatile as they light their Lucky Strikes and thrust out at us huge, glowing sneak-ers made for "urban and suburban beat warriors." Pho-tographs advertising bands, in particular, explicitly evoke images of delinquents from the projects, gangs of unemployed youth hanging out on street corners, often shot from below so that they tower above us, hurl-ing insults, blocking our way, and daring us to pass. CD covers and clothing advertisements often have an underlying plot, that of the ambush, a figurative recreation of a physical confrontation on the streets, where we turn a corner only to find ourselves face to face with the skater-punk band Rancid sprawling against a chain-link fence twisted with barbed wire or with the heavy metal group ProPain standing before the dilapidated shell of an abandoned crack house covered with graffiti. The subtext of many cool ads is imminent attack, a message that takes the saber-rattling defensiveness of urban youth, an attitude with a clear, self-protective purpose, and reduces it to pure style, to a fashionable sulkiness useful in selling tracksuits and CDs.

Coolness offers the disaffected middle class an enticing fantasy, that of going downscale, of descending into abysmal yet liberating poverty, as in the film *Desperately Seeking Susan,* in which a bored housewife, the angst-ridden consort of a wealthy businessman, attempts to alleviate the psychological burden of affluence by modeling herself on the life-force figure of Madonna, a slatternly hedonist who robs her tricks, cadges off her friends, and dries her armpits under restroom hand dryers. And yet the class devolution involved in this odyssey of imaginary indigence presents an extremely stylized vision of destitution, one based, not on austerity, but on conspicuous consumption, on the acquisition of enormous quantities of clothing and kitsch, from bell bottoms, mini-skirts, and go-go boots to snow globes, lava lamps, and ceramic Minnie Mouses. Long stretches of the ultra-cool film *Liquid Sky*, for example, consist of a systematic investigation of the way its demimonde of urbane lowlife—narcoleptic junkies and homicidal androgynes—decorate their squalid hovels, which are crowded with self-parodying displays of thrift store refuse that attest to the characters' contempt for bourgeois tastefulness. In the cool caricature of bohemian life, Mother Hubbard's cupboards are rarely bare but are often crammed with bric-a-brac, with a strangely abundant kind of poverty whose over-accessorized copiousness exposes the fraud of coolness and its Dickensian cult of make-believe mendicancy, a game infused with an ineradicably middle-class sense of comfort. Just as the vision of history behind quaintness is based on a modern concept of abundance, giving rise to the characteristically cluttered look of quaint rooms, so the vision of poverty behind coolness presumes prosperity and the connoisseurship of an eccentric collector who has the leisure and wherewithal to amass tacky curios and far-out knickknacks.

While quaintness often disguises shopping as curating, coolness disguises it as scavenging, as prowling the streets for battered windfalls left at the side of the road, as in Andy Warhol's *Trash*, in which Holly Woodlawn and Joe D'Allesandro comb through garbage cans for salvageable pieces of furniture and chic items of vintage clothing. Shopping in funky boutiques is central to the myth of coolness, which strips consumption of its materialism by portraying it as the ingenious foraging of a new type of inner-city bottom feeder, an urban hunter and gatherer, a discriminating rag-picker who despises brand-new commodities and makes do with serendipitous finds that have no clear provenance, no price tag that identifies their place of origin. Coolness takes the traditional consumer cycle, the rapid decline of a recently purchased article of clothing or appliance from ultra-modern newness to obsolescence, and reverses it, making the waste product itself, not the brand-new acquisition, the valuable commodity, the piece of detritus the coveted fetish item. Even an advertisement for such an archetypal factory-made luxury as a Ford ZX2 capitalizes on the cachet of trash and the myth of the nattily dressed derelict scrounging for retro debris:

Stacy just got a "hip" transplant. And I'm not talking about a medical procedure. See, she bought a new Ford ZX2 and her whole image changed. First she switched her major from Accounting to Graphic Design. Then, she started buying these "funky"' clothes from a second-hand store. Pretty big changes. But I guess we should have seen them coming. Because with a Ford ZX2, you're pretty much telling the world you've decided to excuse yourself from the predictable.

The worship of kitsch is so important to coolness because the hand-me-downs sold in trendy junk shops have been liberated from the stigma of consumerism and the tyranny of the brand-new, thus elevating shopping into an activity of a higher magnitude, that of exhuming priceless artifacts from the bottom of the bargain barrel. Kitsch, in short, is to the hipster what quaintness is to the homeowner: a way of sanitizing consumerism, of endowing it with moral and aesthetic respectability.

While coolness toys with the fiction of grinding poverty, evoking the romance of the scruffy, middle-class pack rat, the creative recycler of orphaned objects, its masquerade of destitution involves an act of

bad faith in that it also fetishizes all of the appurtenances of high technology, the twenty-first-century giz-
mos that its would-be ragamuffins are constantly
pulling out of their backpacks: their cell phones, Mo-
torola pagers, and Pioneer Compact Disc Players. The
company Target claims to specialize in "cool" merchandise, offering everything you need to "transform
your abode into a den of chill repute"—PlayStations,
joy sticks, boom boxes, and stereo systems—electronic
status symbols for the hip young consumer who is
"technologically aggressive and style-progressive, an information addict and an inspector of gadgets." Despite
its pretenses of insolvency, coolness revolves around
the worship of big-ticket items, the very mechanisms
that make the status quo possible. This apparatus of
power represents the most conventional aspects of our
society but has nonetheless become integral to the distinctly futuristic image of the digital dropout, the cyberspace rebel whose coolness inheres in his graceful
mastery of machines, his effortless ability to crack the
codes of ATMs and hack into his high school's computer. Even in Jack Kerouac's *On the Road*, a novel that
is said to have "defined a generation," the suave virility
of his bon vivants is bound up with the distinctly mas-

culine ease with which they operate large vehicles, as in
the case of a parking lot attendant so skilled at his trade
that:

> he can back a car forty miles an hour into a tight
> squeeze and stop at the wall, jump out, race among
> fenders, leap into another car, circle it fifty miles an
> hour in a narrow space, back swiftly into a tight spot

Coolness offers a cartoonish portrait of a technological pastoral, a world we have mastered with our
bravura skills as crackshot engineers. For this reason,
coolness plays a key role in staffing the firms of Silicon
Valley, which revel in a quixotic mystique, promoting
the enticing stereotype of the software designer as a
wizard who magically designs complex inventions inaccessible to the technologically illiterate.

Such novels as *On the Road*, as well as the films of the
French Nouvelle Vague, draw upon another related aspect of coolness: cool tourism, its obsession with aim-
less travel, with the picaresque journeys of rambling
vagabonds constantly on the move, goaded on, not by
curiosity, but by their own internal demons. Direction-
less spiritual odysseys are basic to the narrative of cool

art and advertisements, which celebrate the freedom of the open highway, of a life without responsibilities, the unambitious insouciance of the corporate hobo, as in Sony's ad for its new Discman player, which advises the viewer to "buckle your seatbelts, hit the gas, put in some tunes and don't look back. . . . [Y]ou can rock & roll down that highway called life and never miss a beat. . . . Ahhh, the open road, the wind in your hair, your favorite CDs." These myths of existential tourism, of the wanderlust of rambling itinerants who have rejected the tedium of a settled domestic life for the nomadic existence of a motorized gypsy, have proven especially important for the automobile industry, whose advertisements play upon one of the central fantasies of coolness: of dropping everything, turning one's back on the little cottage with the white picket fence, and speeding away in one's car. Companies such as Ford, Jeep, and Chevrolet describe their evocatively named Mustangs, Wranglers, Renegades, and Rovers as getaway vehicles that enable the staid middle class, the prisoners of monotonous jobs and demanding families, to break loose and roar off into the sunset, leaving in their wake the acrid scent of burned rubber. When Harley-Davidson tells us that "all we know for sure is, the road is infinite," they have turned gas guzzling into a Zen-like meditative state, promoting mindless locomotion as a sedative for bourgeois restlessness and dissatisfaction.

The basic credo of coolness is nihilism, the apocalyptic and somewhat theatrical belief that the American Dream has failed, that success is a trap, that, as one popular hip T-shirt puts it, "life sucks and then you die," a philosophy of affected gloom that suggests that all that matters is the present: getting high, hanging out, indulging the senses, ignoring the rat race. As the Goth rock musician Marilyn Manson has said, "I was a nihilist and now today I'm just too fucking bored." This pretense of anesthetized cynicism inevitably leads to its opposite, to frenzied epicureanism, a carpe diem tendency to equate meaning with pleasure, with the instantaneous gratification of desire. While cool nihilism would seem to represent a wholesale rejection of the materialism of consumer society and its spiritual bankruptcy, in fact it is the ultimate consumerist worldview in that its decimating negativity encourages conspicuous consumption and impulse buying, a permission to purchase stimulated by its transparently literary despair. Nihilism becomes a rationale for consumption, the bitter hatred of the corporate world a license to pamper oneself with its luxuries. The anti-materialism of coolness is thus conveniently expressed in highly materialistic ways.

But hipness is more than just a futile attempt on the part of unglamorous Caucasians to rationalize their extravagance and refashion themselves in the image of brutish proletarians, the "white Negroes" (or, in contemporary Ebonic parlance, the "wiggers") celebrated by Norman Mailer in his seminal 1959 article, in which he stated that, in coolness's "wedding of the white and the black, it was the Negro who brought the cultural dowry." Like the anti-cute, coolness represents a denial of innocence on the part of youth culture, which has begun a full-fledged campaign to accelerate the process of aging in a world in which the demeaning infantilism of childhood has been prolonged well beyond its developmental limits in adolescence. Far from being the threshold of adulthood, puberty still remains mired in the trappings of the nursery, in a sexless limbo in which individuals who have reached physical maturity are nonetheless held captive in their cribs, their sexual impulses kept carefully in check, policed by censorious guardians intent on turning back the hands of their biological clocks. Beginning in the late eighteenth century, the romantic cult of the child resulted in the forcible infantilization of children by over-protective parents, who clung to seraphic visions of their offspring's innocence even as the social conditions in which they were raised were changing dramatically and adolescents spent less and less time jealously sheltered in the bosom of once-insular families, forced instead to fend for themselves on the playgrounds of public schools and in such social organizations as the Boy Scouts and Little League. Coolness represents the final collapse of the romantic movement's adoration of the child, the demise of the religion of innocence, the destruction of sacred tenets of artlessness and chastity hastened by the impatience of sexually informed teenagers fed up with their chimerical status as angelic eunuchs.

The adolescent's rebellion against centuries of child worship takes one of its most violent forms in its extreme humorlessness and its emphatic rejection of the smile, of "niceness," of the amiability of the service economy, which has been supplanted by a sepulchral air of gravity. The typical cool facial expression is not an actual expression so much as a categorical refusal to betray even a hint of a smile, of a desire to please, and the substitution of a mask of characterless nullity, as in the "gangsta" rapper Ice Cube's signature snarl or the unforthcoming rudeness of innumerable bands intent on showing that, far from being cherubs, they are actually ghouls, decades older than their years. The romantic movement's cult of the child has created a foul-mouthed enfant terrible who has turned the playground into a necropolis, where prematurely aged Byronic figures stagger from the merry-go-round to the seesaw to the jungle gym, striking poses of misery and ennui, convinced that their solemnity lends them an air of sophistication and maturity.

Although adolescents would like to believe that the aesthetic of coolness is entirely their own invention, in fact it stems directly from parental hysteria, from the anguished hyperboles of nail-biting moms and dads terrified that their children are drifting toward delinquency, swept up in the recreational drug use and reckless promiscuity of the "wrong crowd." Far from being a fresh and innovative expression of their own culture, coolness is an expression of another culture altogether. It simply brings parental fears to life, providing a grotesque embodiment of a distinctly middle-class projection of freakiness, of what lies beyond the pale of respectable society, where grungy cokeheads with communicable diseases deflower nubile daughters, and the truant sons of upstanding citizens jeopardize their futures by scuffling with the law.

The origin of coolness in the squarest of all possible things, the nightmares of familial worrywarts pacing their living rooms well after curfew, is confirmed by the dependence of cool imagery on highly moralistic caricatures of the demonic and the sacrilegious. Inspired by their love of horror movies, members of the rock group Kiss, for example, assert their coolness by sticking out their bright red tongues dripping with drool and by slathering their faces with cadaverous grease paint, a style of B-grade monster makeup as gruesome as the trademark Bride-of-Frankenstein toilette of Marilyn Manson, who calls himself "Anti-Christ Superstar" and an "Ordained Minister of the Church of Satan." In its effort to scandalize credulous moms and dads, who wring their hands over bad report cards and phone calls from guidance counselors, coolness never succeeds in detaching itself from our society's traditional notions of evil but has created a Halloween aesthetic that conjures up images of abnormality, of an infantile diabolism, refracted through the paranoid parental imagination.

One of the showcases of coolness is the teenager's bedroom, the impenetrable lair of the disgruntled malcontent holed up, in all of his ornery, hormonal testiness, in a dark cave plastered with posters of Puff Daddy and Funk Master Flex. The cool bedroom is not a tasteful nursery painted cheerful colors and equipped with airplane mobiles and shelves of Furbies and Pooh Bears, but a raucous sound studio with speakers the size of refrigerators vibrating with the sounds of Metallica, Neurotica, and Nebula. Such "dens of chill repute" represent an architectural rejection of the whole premise of collectivity on which the nuclear family is based, a solipsistic retreat into the anti-social individuality from which the grouchy teenage crank launches his assault against the same spirit of togetherness that quaintness attempts to preserve. In the film *House Party*, for example, the camera enters the room of a black rapper and, with the alienated objectivity of an anthropologist examining aboriginal artifacts, begins to inspect what its occupant refers to as "my shit," from a stolen road sign stenciled with the suggestive warning "SLIPPERY WHEN WET" to the immense collage of *Penthouse* centerfolds covering the walls from floor to ceiling. Such anti-interior decora-

tion offers an aesthetic affront to the quiet, understated tastefulness of the rest of the house, whose conformity to traditional notions of elegance our sons and
daughters satirize with their self-conscious indecorous-
ness. Despite its seeming nihilism and amorality, coolness is an aesthetic with a mission, a tendentious style
that ridicules the good taste of the suburban split-level,
which it associates with the status quo, with the conventionality of parents who have wasted their entire
lives scrimping and saving to acquire all the necessary
accouterments of respectability. Coolness thumbs its
nose at good taste on moral grounds, inciting a full-
scale aesthetic riot, full of political implications. This
stylistic mutiny demonstrates a surprising streak of
righteous purism by denouncing Mom's immaculate
French Provincial interiors as symptoms of her compli-
ance with the rules of propriety.

One of the appeals of coolness to insecure adolescents is its cultivation of obstreperous ugliness, as in
the case of the musician Rob Zombie who, with a hex
mark carved deeply into his forehead, models himself
on a decomposing corpse, wearing a grizzled, Whit-
manesque beard and a tangled mane of frizzy grey
locks, or Ozzie Osborne, whose face is framed by the

greasy strands of his shoulder-length hair. Part of the success of coolness among self-conscious teenagers stems from the fact that it is so physically forgiving and democratic, so inclusive, rejecting as it does the cookie-cutter aesthetic of "normal" people, of Barbie and Ken, of the voluptuous blond cheerleader and her lantern-jawed, all-American boyfriend. Cool people actively deride conventional notions of physical beauty, associating wholesome, rosy-cheeked good looks with conformity and devoting themselves instead to the cult of the grotesque, which forms a key part of their attack on respectability, on go-getting student council presidents and smugly virtuous teachers' pets, who are polite, presentable, and deferential to their elders. The transformation of the former supermodel Nico from a beauty queen into a scarecrow, a junkie with sinister boiled-egg eyes and rotten teeth, provides an allegory of coolness, which conflates loveliness and elegance with dullness and mediocrity. Nico's defacement of her own beauty to acquire the glamor of coolness shows how the aesthetic of ugliness, like the aesthetic of the teenager's bedroom, is extremely moralistic, based on an almost evangelical contempt for the body, a Gnostic, self-hating puritanism as fanatical as any fringe sect's insistence on the virtue of plainness, severity, and lack of ornament.

Despite the high-handed moralism of the aesthetic of coolness, which is at its most tendentious when it is at its most perverse, youth culture secretly subscribes to the middle-class ethics and sensibility it professes to abhor. One telling indication of the self-contradictory nature of coolness is that, while adolescents persist in believing that they are bad and sinister and unfit for respectable society, the coolest advertisements featuring the hippest kids giving us the dirtiest looks are often selling the cleanest things: pristine white Calvin Klein underpants, immaculate blue jeans, clean sneakers, and sporty colognes. The corporate vision of coolness is inextricably linked with fastidious grooming, with a well-scrubbed subculture whose members' pestilential taint has been eradicated with freshly laundered clothing, deodorant soaps, and a wide variety of shampoos, astringents, and perfumes. (The conventionality of coolness is also revealed in its obsession with such expressions as "strange," "weird," "bizarre," "gross," "wow," and "far-out," exclamations of dismay that reveal that hipness has a distressingly low threshold for the abnormal and that its apparent tolerance for eccentricity masks acute sensitivity to even the subtlest gradations of deviance.)

The hipster not only makes a pigsty of his bedroom and even, despite the prevalence of wholesome advertisements, of his own person, but also engages in noise pollution, in environmental terrorism, another way of defacing the body politic. Breaking the domestic sound barrier with the earsplitting din of car radios and boom boxes becomes a harmless way of disturbing the peace, of shattering the bourgeois tranquillity of bucolic neighborhoods, the ultimate anti-social assertion of the unfettered self. Panasonic even goes so far as to describe its stereo speakers as accessories in these acts of sedition, placing a screaming black teenager next to the words, "Blast it. Crank it. Blare it. Let everyone know you're there. . . . It's louder than your mother." Turning up the volume and blowing the roof off is a symbolic way of destroying property, of rattling windows without breaking them, a form of sonic vandalism that produces the effect of chaos and destruction but nevertheless leaves everything unscathed. Noise, like the affectation of nihilism, constitutes the perfect consumerist rebellion, a clean rebellion, an apolitical radicalism that reduces activism to aesthetics and carefully preserves the world it so blusteringly sets out to destroy.

The centrality of music to the subculture is also related to the Dr. Jekyll and Mr. Hyde aesthetic of coolness. No sooner does the record begin to play than the suave demeanor of the introverted hipster gives way to the rage of the savage beast who, far from being soothed by the proverbially civilizing effects of music, is violently stimulated by them, his composure collapsing on the dance floor into an epileptic flailing of arms and legs. The hero of the movie *Airheads* prides himself on his "quiet cool" until he and his band take to the stage, whereupon they swing their electric guitars like sledgehammers and, amidst showers of sparks, smash their equipment to pieces, all the while screeching the words "degenerate, degenerate," the lyrics of their new hit song. The Janus-faced dichotomy between the primal rock-and-roller and his preternaturally serene daily self reflects the wholesale co-optation of youth culture by the record industry, which has supplied an entire generation with a new opium of the people, with pop music, a type of commercial communication that has supplanted all other forms of social intercourse, such as conversation. The glum taciturnity of coolness represents the tongue-tied silence of a culture that has been rendered mute by its favorite pastime, listening to records and CDs, stricken dumb by the cacophony of superstars whose angry laments prevent conversation, rendering the very need for it superfluous.

The rock band and the inner-city street gang are two of the major inspirations for the look of coolness, which serves a specific sociological function for tightly-knit groups whose very survival depends on their ability to create for the public a unified aesthetic identity. Members of gangs in particular use a complex set of visual symbols to express their allegiance to one another (often sealed through sadistic rites of initiation), from mismatched shoelaces and the position of the belt buckle in relation to the fly to plastic bracelets in coded colors and the menacing hieroglyphs of graffiti that delineate their turf, their sphere of influence. Bands engage in a similar sort of aesthetic demarcation that sets them apart from their competition and creates an instantly recognizable market identity, as can be seen in Korn's matted dreadlocks, Marilyn Manson's gruesomely asymmetrical eyes (cleverly created with color contact lenses), or Kiss's infamous clown makeup, complete with Cowardly Lion whiskers and painted Batman domino masks. Coolness is an aesthetic of trademarks, of the passwords and Masonic handshakes through which card-carrying initiates gain entrance into the clubhouse. Just as affluent youths decontextualize the self-protective surliness of their inner-city peers, so they adopt, like designer labels, the identifying badges of exclusive fraternal societies who create solidarity by wearing black bandannas tied around their thighs or medallions featuring six-pointed stars flanked by flaming pitchforks, emblems that have a specific economic utility, either of mapping out the boundaries of a particular crime syndicate's drug empire or of raising a rock band's profile in a music scene crowded with rivals vying for the media's attention.

But whereas gangs and bands use the aesthetics of insignia to create clannishness on a local level, young people in general use trademarks to create allegiance on an international level, so desperate are they to overcome the barriers that divide them and share in the camaraderie of such groups as the Crips and the Bloods. Coolness has therefore proven to be an enormous boon for manufacturers. If companies like Nike and the Gap can get *their* insignia adopted as the symbol of the pack, *their* "swoosh" trademark, *their* signature leg stripes, *their* headbands decorated with *their* corporate names, they instantly acquire several million freelance advertisers willing to pay for the privilege of spreading the faith and, simultaneously, of achieving visual solidarity by wearing the firm's logo. Clothing is now being explicitly designed, not just with inconspicuous designer labels sewn onto back pockets, but *as* designer labels, with the company's copyrighted art emblems playing an integral part in the garment's design, as in the case of Ralph Lauren's Chap sweatshirts, Benetton's T-shirts, or brands of underwear that feature elastic waistbands as wide as cummerbunds emblazoned with "Joe Boxer," "Yves St. Laurent," and now even "FTL" (Fruit of the Loom). Manufacturers have recognized that the urgent need to create a pack identity in youth culture can easily be used to consolidate corporate identity. In this synergistic relationship, companies provide the products that foster togetherness among the young and the young in turn line the coffers of the CEOs who invent the aesthetic markers that have become the patriotic symbols, the consumerist rallying cries, of teenagers the world over. In a fragmented society in which major institutions like the church and the community no longer play the same role of bringing people together, owning identical possessions becomes one of the chief ways in which we experience community, overcoming our isolation through shared patterns of consumption, communing with each other by acquiring the same cars, Walkmans, and basketball sneakers.

The commercialization of youth culture and the rise, for the first time in history, of a monolithic teenage "look" in most Western countries have intensified the psychological instability of adolescence. The aesthetic divisions between the in-crowd and the out-crowd, so integral to the sociology of the schoolyard, have become even more oppressive as manufacturers begin to use peer pressure as a calculated marketing strategy, setting up shop right out on the basketball court and in the school cafeteria. The victory of the designer label over the playground has led to the ostracism of those who refuse to carry the most fashionable lunch pails or wear this season's de rigueur dungarees, which advertisers portray as keys to acceptance and popularity, ways of preserving peace of mind in a world in which social success requires the systematic elimination of differences with one's peers. It is this uniformity, however, that coolness cleverly disguises as its opposite, as nonconformity, as the rebellion of the nay-saying oddball, the fish out of water, who, even as he suppresses socially unacceptable idiosyncrasies from his personality and reinvents himself in the image of the generic teenager, is magically transformed into an ardent iconoclast for whom shopping becomes nothing less than a subversive form of civil disobedience.

THE ROMANTIC

D uring the heyday of romantic Hollywood films, the cinematic kiss was not a kiss so much as a clutch, a desperate groping whose duration was limited by official censors, who also stipulated that the actors' mouths remain shut at all times, thus preventing even the appearance of French kissing, which was supplanted by a feverish mashing of un-moistened lips. This oddly desiccated contact contrasted dramatically with the clawing fingers of the actresses' hands which, glittering with jewels, raked down their lovers' fully clothed backs, their nails extended like claws, full of aggression and hostility long after the star had thrown caution to the winds, abandoned her shallow pretense of enraged resistance, and succumbed wholeheartedly to her illicit longings. And then, after the ten fleeting seconds allotted by the Legion of Decency had passed, the inopportune entrance of another character often sent them dashing to opposite corners of the room where, their clothing rumpled, their hair a mess, their faces infused with fear, they fiddled with tchotchkes on the mantel or stared pensively at spots in the carpet, retreating into the isolation of their guilty consciences.

This stiff choreography suggests apprehension rather than pleasure, the misgivings of two sexual outlaws who live in a world in which privacy is constantly imperiled, in which doors are forever being flung open, curtains yanked back, and unwanted tea trolleys rolled into occupied bedrooms by indiscreet maids. In an effort to enhance the excitement of the film's plot, the aesthetic of the romantic manufactures an artificial form of paranoia, like that found in Barbara Stanwyck's *Clash By Night,* in which a chain-smoking adulteress and her lover are constantly flinging themselves into each other's arms and then just as quickly wrenching themselves apart at the merest squeak of a floorboard. The romantic pretends that there is far less privacy in the world than there really is, a far greater need for stealth, and evokes a bygone era in which lovers concocted

elaborate schemes to evade the eyes of vigilant chaper-
ones, slipping past watchful mothers who kept guard in
the dark, ready to pounce on wayward daughters for
even minor infractions of their nightly curfews.

As couples began to enjoy the seclusion afforded by
the ambulatory bedrooms of automobiles in the 1920s
and 1930s, as well as by the revolutionary new system of
unsupervised dating, romantic films remained firmly en-
trenched in the past, in a world in which lovers didn't
kiss so much as squeeze the life out of each other, as in
old movie posters representing Kirk Douglas manhan-
dling a sobbing Lana Turner in *The Bad and the Beautiful*
("You're just no good") or Burt Lancaster ravishing Liza-
beth Scott in *I Walk Alone* ("Two things I can handle, baby
. . . guns and dames"). The air of furtiveness, shame, and
conspiracy that enshrouds the cinematic kiss is distinctly
inappropriate in the context of the actual sociology of
sex during the first half of the century, when privacy was
a relatively abundant commodity and couples made out
furiously in the backseats of steamy jalopies on lovers'
lane and the balconies of darkened cinemas while the actors writhing on the screen before them performed with
such anguished compunction what members of the audience did so guiltlessly in their seats.

Old-fashioned Hollywood kisses are carefully arranged compositions that invite the public not only to approach the necking couple but to slip between them and examine at close range every blush and gasp of an act that, on the one hand, optimizes the conditions for viewing and, on the other, makes a bold pretense of solitude, of barring the door to the jealous intruder and excluding the curious stares of gaping au pairs who stumble upon their philandering employers while seeking lost toys in presumably empty rooms. Lovers are frequently filmed in stark silhouette against a white background so that, for purposes of visual clarity, their bodies don't obscure each other: a bulging forearm blocking from view a famous face; the broad rim of a stylish chapeau, a magnificent set of eyes brimming with desire—a cinematic feat of separation similar to that performed by pornographers, who create a schematic type of televisual sex by prying their actors so far apart that they are joined, like Siamese twins, at the point of penetration alone. Greta Garbo's *Camille* is one of the masterpieces of the choreographed kiss; wracked by ominous bouts of consumptive hacking, she frequently falls into Robert Taylor's manly arms, collapsing into a boneless swoon in which her head tips back so far that her nose points directly up at the ceiling, as if, in the heat of passion, she had somehow broken her neck, while her lover hovers above her, reveling in her passivity.

Once the Hollywood kiss is finished, the camera often pivots to the man's back, where the radiant face of the leading lady is shown in all of its dazzling, dewy-eyed euphoria in the over-the-shoulder shot, which provides the audience direct access to the internal state of the kisser, the tumultuous desires that are projected on a screen within a screen: the actress's troubled brow, heavily lidded eyes, and sultry, pouting lips. To make the kiss as emotionally legible as possible, the starlet's leg often bends at the knee and rises involuntarily in the polite, Production Code equivalent of an erection, a reflexive gesture that provides a physical manifestation of an unfilmably subjective response, as if her rapture were so transcendent that she had begun to levitate—a convention that still has a certain limited currency, as can be seen in Woody Allen's *Crimes and Misdemeanors,* in which Angelica Houston kisses her lover while performing for the viewer the obligatory leg lift, a gesture meant to demonstrate, not helpless arousal, but the romantic fatuity of the character she is playing. While actors seem to make love in a state of privacy heightened by the sadistic plots of the villainous puritans who seek to expose them, they are in fact flagrant exhibitionists who delight in hamming up their lust for the new mass audience, which forces the camera into the exact center of their intimacy, the empty white space between their silhouetted faces, a vacancy that is in fact quite full, occupied by an entire auditorium of prurient spectators. The Hollywood kiss embodies a central paradox of the way consumerism and its cultural industries represent romance, which is portrayed as both a gregarious activity and a reclusive one, at once convivial and covert, a stage show put on for the benefit of others and an anxious struggle to regain the privacy we have lost as our love lives have been commercialized, transformed into occasions for the public display of our assets and purchasing power.

The implicit presence of the audience reflects the extraordinary changes that have occurred in courtship rituals in the course of the twentieth century, which has seen the emergence of an historically unprecedented type of encounter between the sexes: the date. Before the twentieth century, there were no dates, no lavish nights on the town in which men shelled out an entire month's wages for corsages, highballs at Delmonico's, five-course meals at the 21 Club, tickets for Broadway plays, and waltzes on the sixty-fifth floor of the Rainbow Room. Potential suitors met women on their own turf, in their parents' parlors, where they sat in stiff-backed chairs self-consciously sipping tea and nibbling scones under the hawkish eye of protective mothers, who regaled their guests with a soothing patter of cultivated generalities. Only in the first quarter of the century did "calling" give way to "dating," a response in part to the predicament of the urban proletariat who, crowded into dilapidated tenements whose seedy flats consisted of one or two multi-purpose rooms, had no parlor in which to woo and therefore sought refuge in the public sector, everywhere from the speakeasy and the dance hall to the drive-in diner and the drugstore soda fountain, where the stern supervision of disapproving parents was replaced by the equally inquisitive meddlesomeness of the couple's peers.

The shift of the setting for courtship from the domestic world to the commercial sphere created a whole new consciousness of the watching public and radically altered both the economics and the aesthetics of seduction, creating an atmosphere of intense competition in which suitors were forced to prove their worth through their ability to buy sixteen-stone Cartier bracelets, bottles of Dom Perignon, and gifts of Odalisque Eau De Parfum Fashion Mist. The modern aesthetic of the romantic, while borrowing freely from chivalrous and Ovidian clichés of mischievous Cupids darting about thunder-heads, moons that "dance in the sky" while "all the stars turn into diamonds," white knights jousting on rearing steeds, and helpless damsels swooning on crenellated turrets, is deeply rooted in the dramaturgy of the date, in the gamesmanship of a commercial encounter that is less than a century old. The aesthetic assumed its modern form when men and women fled from their parents' houses and entered an arena crowded with other lovers who used bouquets of roses ("perfect with wine on a moonlit night") and boxes of Godiva Chocolates ("who needs Cupid?") as ammunition for preemptive strikes. No longer was flirtation insulated from consumerism, taking place in a room without a cash register—the parlor—well outside the fray of fern bars and discotheques, where jealous contenders use aggressive, adversarial tactics to vanquish their sexual competitors, vying to create the perfect evening, whose material excesses are motivated by sheer one-upsmanship.

The porch swing and the hay ride figured prominently in nineteenth-century iconography representing relations between the sexes. The unabashedly theatrical setting most closely associated with contemporary romance, by contrast, is the dinner table, the central prop of romantic images in advertisements for everything from contraceptives to sanitary napkins, all of which rely heavily on soft-focused shots of happy couples clicking glasses bubbling with champagne. The incongruous new dependence of lovemaking on the act of eating and drinking reflects the displacement of the living room by the restaurant as the chief forum for seduction. This commercial establishment now dominates our fantasies of true love, despite the fact that there is nothing intrinsically intimate about the act of chewing and swallowing food, of mopping up pools of coagulating gravy with hunks of bread and sinking one's teeth into meaty drumsticks. Companies repeat the motif of the restaurant so frequently that, in many advertisements, they use a kind of pictorial shorthand in which all that is shown is the table itself: the candle, the rose, the half-empty wine goblets, the ice-cold soda with two straws, the burning cigarettes (one with a lipstick stain, as in the ad for Camel Special Lights). The principal players of this romantic ghost town have mysteriously disappeared and all that remains is the real point of the aesthetic, the merchandise itself. The immaculate, linen-covered table is the symbolic icon of the mercantilization of courtship and one of the primary locations for flirting in the movies, as in Cher's *Moonstruck,* in which couples bicker, break up, dash drinks in each other's faces, and then propose on bended knee as the maitre d' swoops in and out with a wine bottle and a heavily laden dessert cart trundles past. Flickering with votive candles and adorned with a modest bud vase, this unassuming piece of furniture is the very altar for the modern aesthetic of flirtation, the sacrificial dais on which lovers offer up their weekly paychecks, winning their way into each others' hearts amidst the distractions of hunger, the nuisance of greasy fingers, the inevitability of spills, and the potential hazard of sharp utensils. Far from being a place of relaxation and enjoyment, the restaurant table, unlike the porch swing, is the theater of operations for a Darwinian struggle for survival in which hordes of rival contestants jockey for the spotlight in what one sociologist has called the "rating and dating system," a type of seduction by means of economically engineered ambiance.

Modern romance aestheticizes not only public assignations like dinners at restaurants but the out-of-doors in general, the setting for the most romantic scenes of such movies as *Love Story*, in which Ali McGraw and Ryan O'Neil pelt each other with snowballs in Harvard Yard while ethereal music plays in the background, or *It Could Happen to You*, in which Nicholas Cage is so captivated by the beautiful woman rollerblading by his side that he overshoots his mark and plunges waist-deep into a lake. In advertisements as well, the act of courtship has become nothing less than a contact sport in which scantily clad men and women, tossing footballs and smashing each other with pillows, are shown howling with laughter as they run piggyback through the surf, douse each other with garden hoses, and make gravity-defying leaps to catch Frisbees, so exhilarated are they to be smoking Menthol Lights and drinking Snapple ice tea. Romantic images no longer feature staid bachelors in swallow-tailed coats politely tipping their top hats to ladies with parasols but instead half-naked savages in Bermuda shorts and bathing suits who, hyperventilating with uncontrollable hilarity, spar like professional boxers and ride on each other's shoulders displaying to the camera silky smooth legs that have "got to be Nair legs."

Nature has always served as one of the primary aesthetic backdrops of romance because being out in the open offered greater opportunities for seclusion than being indoors. It was once far easier for couples to find solitude in parks, gardens, and labyrinths of topiary hedges than in the inviting yet perilous privacy of houses, where supervision was much more tightly controlled and where feverish confessions of amorous feelings were more incriminating than if lovers lingered on a park bench, snuck into a gazebo in an arboretum, or straggled behind their party for impromptu tête-à-têtes during postprandial promenades. The unthinkable possibility of being caught alone in a room drove people out-of-doors into a morally neutral zone, ironically seeking protection in places of exposure, in playgrounds teeming with excited members of the Pepsi Generation and swimming pools surrounded by people sunbathing in Coppertone and toasting each other with tumblers full of Jim Beam Bourbon. This banishment into wide open spaces has left a permanent mark on the aesthetic of the romantic which, in everything from greeting cards to calendars, represents couples dwarfed by the immensity of nature, sitting on docks bathed in the light of sunsets and standing on the edges of dizzying precipices contemplating panoramic views of snow-capped peaks, as in an ad for Advil in which two windblown lovebirds cavort on a yacht as the woman silently asks herself, "what cramps?" As the divorce rate steadily rises, however, and even the most traditional couples are at best serial monogamists, the association of courtship with sublime vistas of picturesque scenery takes on an urgent new meaning: The immutability of nature seems to affirm the permanence of ever more *im*permanent relationships. Advertisers transform even the most transient of flings into lifelong commitments by placing couples in a distinctly allegorical landscape where, wafting clouds of bewitching designer fragrances and taking deep drags on cigarettes, they scale alpine heights and trudge through deep canyons that suggest emotional ties as enduring, as impregnable to the vagaries of modern life, as the rock formations around them.

The central conceit of the unchanging landscape has a second allegorical meaning. An advertisement for Dockers Khakis featuring lovers painstakingly constructing a sand castle on the shore or for Newport cigarettes depicting two tipsy revelers blowing party favors in each other's faces presents a pastoral utopia in which all rivals have been ruthlessly liquidated through a type of aesthetic genocide. The greeting card industry's favorite Valentine images of perennially itinerant couples forever walking over sand dunes, playfully kicking through piles of autumn leaves, and wading through snowdrifts are based on a recurrent fantasy: Lovers are portrayed as refugees from their own kind, ostracized and oppressed by society at large, which has been eliminated from romantic advertisements, creating eerily unpopulated spaces, the echoing ruins of a civilization that the aesthetic wipes out as effectively as the neutron bomb. The iconography of empty landscapes, in which couples stand alone in an Edenic wilderness, seemingly the last people on Earth, like the lovers featured on the can of Arrid Extra Dry standing face-to-face silhouetted against a sunset, reflects a deep-seated misanthropy, an anti-social cynicism that allows couples to seal themselves in the hermetic world of their own monastic fidelity, insulated from their families and peers, defying the malicious gossip of homeroom busybodies and the irate admonitions of distraught parents. While romance has always exhibited symptoms of misanthropy, satirizing the old-fashioned prejudices of our elders, à la "Romeo and Juliet," the fact that seduction has become less private, more dependent on displays of conspicuous consumption, and more rooted in the cutthroat competition of dating, has generated an even greater sense of exasperation with a society that operates like a sexual police force, able to scrutinize every move lovers make now that the ordeal of courtship takes place out in the open, in bars and restaurants.

Companies used images of embracing couples to sell their products as early as the 1920s, when the aesthetic of the romantic made its debut as one of the dominant looks of twentieth-century advertisements, which rely heavily on fairy-tale scenes of intimate encounters in luxurious settings that produce, as a Miss Lonelyhearts columnist called it, that "warm fuzzy glow in the pit of your stomach." The earliest ads didn't entice, they threatened, as can be seen in a whole genre of heartbreaking cartoons that appeared in major magazines well into the 1960s. One features a crestfallen housewife standing penitent before a bullying husband, who shakes a tasteless sandwich in her face, promising divorce, until, in the next frame, her marriage foundering, she rushes out and buys him "spicy, satisfying" Underwood Deviled Ham, which he finds so scrumptious that he sweeps her off her feet and places her on his lap, where she pops tasty morsels into his mouth, her home life the picture of cozy contentment. Similarly, a 1940 advertisement for Ipana Toothpaste represents a disastrous evening at a restaurant, where a woman dressed to the nines, her eyes lowered humbly as her paramour is about to pose the question, destroys her prospects for a happy marriage when she flashes him a grimacing, jack-o'-lantern smile: "She had always hoped it would happen this way—soft lights, smooth music, his eyes speaking volumes: 'You're beautiful,' they said, 'beautiful.' But then—she smiled! And his eagerness gave way to indifference. For beauty is always dimmed and darkened under the cloud of a dull and dingy smile." Companies characterized their products as essential to the very outcome of courtship, which was constantly jeopardized by yellow teeth, dry skin, bad breath, wretched cooking, grey hair, premature wrinkles, weak coffee, bristly chins, and, most insidiously of all, "the goat beneath the arm," which could be tamed only by Madame Berthé's Zip Cream Deodorant, a spring-fresh antiperspirant that, according to the advertisement's fat, drowsy Cupid, "makes my job easy." Manufacturers used images of romantic triumphs both to instill fears of humiliating failure and to offer hopes of instantaneous success by setting themselves up as gypsy potion makers, the palm-reading purveyors of such love philters as Pepsodent, which gives you "man power," or Olga Girdles, which cause men to stop dead in their tracks as women with hour-glass figures poured into slinky, skin-tight dresses stride disdainfully by.

By the 1960s, the causal relation that manufacturers once posited between, on the one hand, the ecstatic bride-to-be gazing entranced at the rock her fiancée slips on her finger at Tiffany's and, on the other hand, the bottle of mouthwash, the box of Fels-Naptha Soap Chips, and the package of Modess tampons, had become too absurdly literal for an increasingly educated consumer fully aware of the false promises of advertisements that stated in no uncertain terms that marital satisfaction could be purchased—as well as ruinous divorces averted—for pennies. As Madison Avenue and the public matured, manufacturers invented a new aesthetic. They began to use images of romantic happiness in a much more figurative way that refrained from browbeating consumers with cautionary tales about "dateless Dotties," forsaken flops with halitosis and dandruff parked before telephones that never ring. Instead, the relation between the shopper's sexual conquests and her purchases became much more implicit, the hectoring tone disappeared, and advertisements revolved around an idealized vision of the good life, presenting products in close conjunction with visually compelling photographs of laughing couples. Mere contiguity replaced badgering causality and viewers were left to draw for themselves the connection between the voluptuous aesthetics of an intimate romantic scene and the miracles of Jiffy, Jergen's, or Nair.

Instead of scolding us with homilies about loveless pariahs, the aesthetic of the romantic was suddenly about having "fun," about the stress-free hedonism of affluent lovers vacationing in tropical resorts surrounded by groves of swaying palms and "tranquil lagoons of azure blue" where they snorkeled by coral reefs, indulging in a joyous epicureanism. Femstat 3, a medication for yeast infections, advertises its product with an irresistible image of a laughing black couple, while Diet Coke dispenses with the old tendentiousness altogether and represents a man and woman whooping it up above a caption that reads, "Laughter is a great workout. Got a taste for fun? Don't just talk about it— get together! Applaud the sunset, dance the night away." It was Clairol, however, that invented the classic "fun" ad, the perfect expression of the new philosophy of joie de vivre that sells products through images of an entirely unedifying type of self-gratification: "Is it true blondes have more fun? . . . Doors open for blondes. Traffic stops for blondes. Men adore you, do more for you, life is tops for blondes! So switch to bewitch!"

The highly stylized type of romantic happiness presented in modern advertisements is often extremely inequitable. It frequently shows the man far more involved than the woman, with his face nestled in a lustrous mane of pH-balanced, hypoallergenic hair set with a volumizing mousse, while *her* gaze is locked on the reader in a look of complicitous triumph, like the seductress on the box of the *Better Sex Video Series,* who looks out at us as if she were entirely unaware that her lover is nibbling frantically on her ear. The aesthetic of romance creates images of women as rapacious carnivores lazily pawing their prey, as in an advertisement from the early 1960s for Vis à Vis perfume by Helena Rubinstein featuring a woman who winks at us as her infatuated admirer snaps a necklace as heavy as the crown jewels around her neck, a propitiatory gift she snagged because "she never played fair. For example, that fragrance she used. It was very new. It was very wicked. And it broke all our rules. . . . It isn't fair but it works." Madison Avenue's aesthetics of true love create portraits of sated Circes who, having successfully captured their quarry, do not revel in the affection they feel for their devotees but instead seek to open up communication with the viewer and reassure her that "it works," that she too can enslave her man. The result is an uncanny and, under circumstances meant to suggest emotional closeness, entirely inappropriate picture of female disengagement, an abstracted look of introspection, of aloofness, of unbridgeable distance between the slave and the uninvolved femme fatale, who experiences greater intimacy with the audience than with her victim.

The aesthetic of the romantic is based on an austere and conventional body of images as rigidly iconographic as Byzantine art. This radically simplified pictorial language consists of only a handful of recurrent symbols: hearts pierced by arrows, cherubic Cupids, ceramic picture frames surrounded by wreaths of "XOXOXO hugs and kisses" that capture "that swept-away-in-the-moment-feeling," advertisements of couples toasting each other over cinnamon-scented candles, and clusters of Mylar balloons that "are sure to bring a smile, and possibly a tear, to that special someones [sic] face." The assumption behind the repetitiveness of the aesthetic is that love is such a universal experience that it reduces us all to the same generic person, the same beach-walker, the same sunset-admirer, who relies on the same commercially manufactured images of intimacy: marshmallows roasting over an open fire, corks popping out of champagne bottles, the soaring scores of late night tearjerkers, or nine-carat diamond rings that a bride-to-be "can safely describe as 'that's me!'" The romantic is an aesthetic of commonality, and its mawkishness, its unoriginality, are both endearing and intrinsic to its appeal. This lovable triteness suggests a basic failure of imagination, an inability to be original in the face of a disarmingly intense experience that infantilizes us, turning us into tongue-tied Romeos who express our feelings through culturally sanctioned formulae whose corniness provides a peculiar testament to the strength of our inarticulate passion.

The notion that desire is a great leveler, that it renders us speechless and inept and thus forces us to rely on mood-enhancing commodities to capture the attention of our partners, is particularly useful for consumerism, which generously offers to bale us out and stage-manage our intimate moments, to decorate the theatrical setting for seduction with all of the requisite props: tranquil sounds of easy-listening music, the cloying aroma of sandalwood incense, and "luscious hazelnut delicacies," each of which comes wrapped with "a love note." Manufacturers have profited immensely from the topos of romantic ineloquence by pretending to come to our rescue as the ghost writers of our billet doux who, by means of greeting card limericks and prepackaged "Gentle Kiss" gift baskets of bath oils, soaps, and scents, express sentiments we are taught to believe we are too uncouth, too graceless, to express for ourselves ("let *us* do the talking for you"). Consumerism actively strives to undermine our confidence in our skills at seduction so that we will feel compelled to rent the services of the love industry, the seemingly magnanimous peddlers of bouquets of roses from 1–800-FLORIST, Hawaiian getaways, Internet e-mail "digital hugs," and "delightfully girlie relationship cards" that read "sweetheart, I'm like the rose and you're like the early drops of water on my petals." What's more, consumerism strengthens our dependence on the artificial aesthetic of romance by enlisting the help of the human potential movement, which insists that, to maintain healthy "intrapersonal" relationships, we must constantly express our affection, that we must shower each other with gifts and, at the risk of being branded emotional cripples, affirm our bonds in a flamboyant and extroverted fashion, doing such things as taking our lovers on trips to Fiji where, with "the warm turquoise sea lapping your toes," we can "swap the hustle and bustle for a taste of Nirvana." Pop psychology thus helps create an atmosphere of compulsory demonstrativeness in which we are required to make periodic confessions of our feelings through tokens of our esteem, an obsessive communicativeness that has increased the materialism of courtship ten-fold. A society more restrained about repeating declarations of eternal devotion would not be as naively reliant as we have become on the booming service economy of the love industry.

And yet the contrived conventionality of the romantic is at war with the basic philosophy of consumerism: that we must strive to be different, unique, rebels whose touchingly ineffectual insurrection consists of shopping to differentiate ourselves from the mass market. The deliberately democratic aesthetic of seduction has thus been invaded by another aesthetic, by zaniness, which allows lovers to rise above the lowest common denominator and exhibit their nonconformity even while flirting, an activity whose essential purpose is to make us all alike, to eliminate our differences and highlight our shared humanity. Greeting card companies now divide their stock into such categories as "wacky," "sassy," and "salacious" and feature images that actively satirize saccharine poetic conventions with messages that read, "I love you to pizzas"; cartoon caricatures of trolls in black socks, garter belts, and raincoats who win their ladyloves by flashing them on subway platforms; or pictures of wedding cakes accompanied by lines of playful doggerel: "I can't live without you./I'd climb the highest mountain,/Swim the deepest ocean./Did I mention I'm rich?" Hollywood comedies also belabor the eccentricities of their lovelorn protagonists and counteract the sentimentality of archaic romance plots by providing a heavy dose of slaphappy kookiness, as in the film *Happy Together*, in which two infatuated college students ride across campus on wobbling unicycles, roller skate through the library, drink champagne in an inflatable wading pool in their dorm room, and eat candy out of a doggy bowl.

No longer do we seduce each other through lugubrious displays of downcast solemnity, but rather through the deliriously batty antics of stand-up comedians who reject the dehumanizing conventions of romance for the madcap vivacity of a presumably adorable nuttiness. Playing the oddball, the misfit, or what the book *Guerrilla Dating Tactics* calls "a frisky adult willing to embrace a crazy moment" helps us escape the limitations of such a conformist aesthetic as the romantic, which, in an era that clings to the illusion of its individuality, is embroiled in an iconographic civil war.

The unmitigated goofiness of a cigarette advertisement that depicts two lovers spraying each other with shaving cream is often indistinguishable from the spirit of bathos that now reigns in contemporary romantic comedy, a maliciously gleeful delight in the incongruous, a zest for deflating accidents, for inebriated best men who splash into punch bowls, orgiastic bachelor parties in which the betrothed falls head over heels for the hired entertainment, and lavishly catered receptions that disintegrate into food fights between feuding clans. Two pivotal props of romantic films play a central role in subverting the well-oiled machinery of storybook nuptials: the bridal gown and the toothbrush.

Hollywood has declared war on the immaculate hymeneal veil, which has become nothing less than the canvas for a kind of action painting. During a series of humiliating traumas as destructive as the mishaps that demolish automobiles in zany films, the dress is reduced to a wet, tattered rag—stained, burned, and ripped by cat fights with rivals, drunken tumbles into swimming pools, and embarrassing encounters with ferocious dogs that play slobbering games of tug-of-war with priceless lace trains. The wedding party filmed in the 1989 movie *True Love* begins triumphantly with the bride and groom slow-dancing while waiters carrying baked Alaskas and cakes with sparklers circle around them but ends on a less victorious note, with the angry bride sitting astride a toilet in a public restroom, sulking in a stall, her dress dragging on the dirty, wet floor. The vandalized bridal gown is the sacrificial emblem on which we take out our frustrations with the inhibiting formalities of wooing, an effigy we use to purge ourselves of social customs that have lost their meaning even as they have become more expensive, with engagement rings claiming at least two months' salary and "honeymoon lingerie" costing $500 for a lace bodice and a matching thong.

Similarly, the toothbrush demolishes the fictions surrounding the ostensibly idyllic pleasures of cohabitation. Couples in films are increasingly forced to submit to the humiliating rigors of a new aesthetic of anti-climax, best seen in what might be called the toothbrush test, an iconic moment in romantic comedies in which anxious newlyweds appear together in the bathroom bereft of glamor, spitting peppermint foam into the sink and flossing their teeth. One of the crucial romantic scenes of Richard Gere and Julia Roberts's *Pretty Woman* focuses on an arm wrestling match over a pack of dental floss, while the impetuous multi-racial lovers in *Fools Rush In* have some of their tenderest moments fighting plaque and odor-causing bacteria at the same sink. Extravagantly unflattering portrayals of dental hygiene present an entirely uncommercialized vision of romance, a de-aestheticized vision, an antidote to the connubial bliss represented in advertising. The commercialization of courtship in the course of the twentieth century has led to a backlash against the crass materialism of fairy-tale romance, creating an anti-aesthetic that attempts to sever, once and for all, the intimate connection between love and money. Like the anti-cute, bathos serves a therapeutic function, that of cleansing us of a mercenary aesthetic whose antiquated conventions—so crucial for the livelihoods of jewelers, florists, travel agents, real estate brokers, bakers, balloon vendors, and bubble bath manufacturers—cause psychological anguish and seldom strengthen intimacy as they promise, failing entirely to ward off the grim realities of loneliness.

ZANINESS

I n the opening scene of one of the masterpieces of zaniness, *The Naked Gun,* a black
detective sneaks aboard a ship docked in a
Los Angeles harbor, tiptoes across the deck, and then
whips open a cabin door to reveal a group of dissipated
desperadoes sitting around a table. They are the king-
pins of a nefarious ring of cocaine traffickers, who draw
their guns in unison and riddle his flailing body with
bullets. Rather than crumpling to the floor, he performs an elaborately choreographed death scene in
which he reels across the room in the protracted agony
of a saloon cowboy, clutching his bleeding chest and
leaving in his wake a path of destruction that involves
an exasperatingly familiar set of sight gags. He first
slams his head into a pipe, then burns his hand on a

potbellied stove, slithers down a wall marked "Wet Paint," crushes his fingers in a window, collapses face-first into a wedding cake, and lurches into a bear trap. Only then does he make a graceless and belated exit overboard, having run an obstacle course booby-trapped with the conventions of a style of humor that violates the most elementary rules governing the sanctity of the human body.

Zaniness is so basic to popular culture that it forms a fundamental part of the very look of our daily lives. Relying more on physical gaffs and pratfalls than on witty conversation, on gestures and facial expressions than on punch lines, it pervades everything from *Sesame Street* and the Muppets to Saturday morning cartoons and *Mad Magazine*, from the Three Stooges and the Marx Brothers to *Ren and Stimpy* and *Beavis and Butt-Head*, the protagonists of a new generation of smart-aleck MTV and Nickelodeon programs that experiment with the grotesque manipulation of their animated characters' disturbingly malleable forms.

What gives contemporary zaniness its maniacal edge is, in part, a dramatic escalation in the sheer quantity of humorous material that we encounter around us: Far Side desk calendars, flying-toaster screen savers, pencil sharpeners lodged in the nostrils of plastic noses, comic strips in which anvils plummet out of windows onto the unsuspecting heads of innocent passersby, and computer software that plays jingles from Warner Brothers' Looney Tunes. This slaphappy spirit has penetrated into the very fabric of the twentieth century, into our clothing, appurtenances, and utensils, things that have never been the vehicles for humor before. The modern landscape is littered with vast stockpiles of ludicrous paraphernalia, which we arrange like shrines in our kitchens, bedrooms, and offices.

In a society intolerant of unconventional behavior, we have devised a symbolic method of achieving the illusion of rebelliousness by practicing controlled nonconformity. Zaniness allows us to misbehave and yet minimizes our risk of being ostracized as eccentric. It is based not on real individuality but rather on the harmless iconoclasm of the typical prankster, who delights in edible fake snot, farting teddy bears, and "Barf Man" masks whose chins dribble with plastic vomit, the sort of merchandise found in the three house organs of zaniness: the Archie McPhee Collector's Edition Catalog, the Things You Never Knew Existed Catalog, and the Chicken Boy Catalog for a Perfect World. In these cultish mail order circulars, the models are dressed in such "witty wearables" as rubber chicken heads, T-shirts stenciled with the words "Thank you for *not* projectile vomiting," shark fin shower caps, "cat in space" brooches, and wacky sweatshirts that the advertising copy announces "silently scream, 'hey, I'm a nut!'"

All three catalogs celebrate noncomformity through the acquisition of inanimate objects that convey to others the false impression of unruliness and autonomy. The consumer uses this innocuous disobedience to convince himself that he is a kooky, pleasantly maladjusted oddball, the proverbial square peg in the round hole. Only a culture with a ruthlessly prescriptive notion of what constitutes normality could foster an aesthetic that functions as a preposterous caricature of *ab*normality, of the weird, the off-the-wall, a notion that allows even the most staid individuals, simply by wearing squirting eyeballs or Fido Dido "Normal is Boring" T-shirts, to pretend to themselves that they are loose cannons in a world paralyzed by the inhibitions of propriety. Such items as pickles that squeak or talking toilet seats that scream out when you sit on them "can't you see I'm working down here?" reveal that zaniness is the highly stylized way in which a conventional culture imagines deviance and marginality, which it represents through an aesthetic that transforms real eccentricities into an essentially benign form of playfulness. Zaniness comprises the artistic and cinematic conventions through which we absorb and neutralize disturbing differences of behavior and attitude, which we caricature through the medium of popular culture, through cartoons, comic strips, and films in which the unsocialized weirdness of the extremist and the heretic becomes something altogether less threatening, less destabilizing to the status quo.

Controlled nonconformity is practiced in a variety of other ways aside from exploding golf balls or audiotapes that play "over 140 authentic burps" ("experience complete hysteria," the catalog tells us, "as you and your friends listen to rude, unusual, long and loud gastrointestinal eruptions"). Zaniness is an extremely invasive aesthetic, having spread into our conversations, which are now scripted like *Cheers* or *Married with Children*, programs whose frenetic rhythms have affected our speech, transforming our encounters with our friends and co-workers into rapid-fire exchanges of repartee. In our efforts to devise for ourselves a social mask that suggests whimsical yet acceptable individuality, we are so faithful to the formulaic structure of sit-coms, the inflexible alternation of hard-hitting wise-cracks and stunning rejoinders, that our conversations often amount to nothing more than recreations of the snappy patter of prime-time TV. During fits of sparring, we toss off extemporaneous lines that seem to have been plagiarized from nightly episodes of our favorite programs and even take turns impersonating for each other the studio audience, issuing our own version of canned laughter, the unspontaneous titters with which we ceremonially greet people's efforts to be witty.

This forced spirit of madcap merriment has affected the modern office where controlled nonconformity flourishes in an atmosphere of suppressed delirium that manifests itself, not only in the salty humor with which office workers decorate their desks, but in the relentless facetiousness with which they address each other. This oppressive battiness, replete with double entendres, forms the secret handshake of a new zany camaraderie, the formal salute with which office workers, eager to test but not cross the limits of acceptable behavior, express solidarity against the business environment, which they undermine with an entirely innocuous form of humor brimming with ineffectual rage against the mandates of rationality and professionalism.

Both office humor and such spectacles as sit-coms, which essentially function for their audiences as laughter vomitoriums, offering a wisecrack once every ten seconds, also reflect a fundamental shift in our attitudes towards the uses of comedy. Whereas making jokes was once a form of recreation, we have now elevated it from a pastime into a form of therapy, a way of invigorating our treasured illusions of rebelliousness and of counteracting the forces of "negativity." Such pessimism not only contradicts the ideals instilled in us by a service economy, which places a high value on maintaining cordial customer relations, but is the central target of the human potential movement, which has taught us that the failure to cultivate a "positive" attitude causes everything from cancer to demotions, from unpopularity to divorce. Because humor has been converted into a crucial part of our culture's psychological hygiene, we now produce and consume vast amounts of unnecessary laughter with the same spirit of self-punishing discipline with which we undertake austere regimens of dieting and exercise. We induce laughter much as bulimics induce vomiting, to fulfill the harsh ultimatums of a new comic agenda that force-feeds us enormous amounts of silliness, which we use like emetics to cleanse ourselves of our solemnity, emerging from these heaving convulsions of false merriment fresh, upbeat, "perky." Terrified by the consequences of not participating in this rite of mass hilarity, we now pursue comedy with a kind of aggression and self-persecuting single-mindedness foreign to societies in which laughter serves the modest function of providing amusement rather than helping us to heal, advance our careers, or find a mate. Zaniness is thus as full of dread as it is of delight. It has more in common with fear than it does with enjoyment.

The inexorable spread of zaniness represents a uniquely modern moment, that of life imitating art, and thus provides concrete evidence of something we are constantly trying to document but that eludes the best efforts of even the most accomplished sociologists: the effect of the mass media on everyday life. This issue preoccupies many social commentators, who are disturbed by the gratuitous sadism of television violence and its influence on the young, a conundrum that is far more puzzling than the blatant ways in which television zaniness has permeated our lives, wreaking far greater havoc on its victims than the daily dose of carnage they consume while watching *L.A. Law* and *Miami Vice*. New forms of mass entertainment are now exerting such strong pressure on how we act that we bear on our faces and in our gestures the imprint of what we watch on the screen, taking with us, out of the cineplex and into the workplace, unnatural styles of behavior that were concocted expressly for Hollywood goofball farce.

Because zaniness can be defined as a by-product of a culture suffused with mass entertainment, the best way to understand the effect of controlled nonconformity on the hordes of ordinary people who are now remaking themselves in the images of such lively clowns as Steve Martin, Lily Tomlin, Jim Carey, and Pee Wee Herman is to examine its origins in cinema and to look at the way in which popular comedy has developed over the course of the last fifty years. The boisterous and unapologetically puerile style of zaniness is not a new development within the context of modern humor; it has evolved from a remarkably stable comic tradition that has essentially remained the same for centuries, from the cartwheels and somersaults of the commedia dell'arte to the stylized violence of the Keystone Cops. Recently, however, the conventions of this type of broad humor have undergone an extraordinary transformation. Zaniness is the product of a series of mutations that occurred within crude physical farce under the influence of new social conditions that have irrevocably altered our perception of the meaning and use of humor.

Slapstick, the cinematic tradition from which zaniness evolved, interacted explosively with the rise of consumerism to produce an aesthetic whose berserk style was quickly incorporated into the comic persona we assume when we converse and flirt. Zaniness shares one crucial feature with the history of both low comedy in general and slapstick in particular: its central joke—its treatment of the body as an inanimate object, as in the opening scene of *The Naked Gun,* which depicts a typical zany martyrdom of a character who is forced to run the gauntlet of goofball's most popular gimmicks. The paradox of the human object lies behind everything from the silent comedian's concussive blows and crippling spills down steep flights of stairs to the film *Weekend at Bernie's,* whose central character, a millionaire embezzler brutally murdered in the beginning of the film, is dragged around like a rag doll through scenes that involve macabre acts of corpse desecration by two Wall Street yuppies, who staple his toupee to his skull and prop him up in sunglasses on a lawn chair. Popular comedy has always been closely associated with morbidity, with a distinctly ghoulish curiosity about the body's capacity to withstand suffering. It is rooted, not in pleasure, but in pain, not in laughter, but in the rictus grin, the characteristic expression of clenched teeth with which the zany hero is buffeted through so many American comic strips and films, surviving only by virtue of his body's uncanny resilience and miraculously recuperative powers, which enable him to emerge unscathed after diving through plate-glass windows and smashing into fruit stands. Like *The Road Runner's* luckless villain, who is constantly skidding over precipices, being squashed by Mack trucks, and burned to a cinder by bundles of prematurely exploding TNT, the zany protagonist becomes the butt of a series of pranks in which he is ritualistically beaten, crushed, and then, invariably, blasted into the air as a living cannon ball, which, in turn, caroms into yet another body, setting in motion a chain reaction of ever more violent collisions.

In their purest form, zany comedies are structureless, picaresque journeys through worlds of dangerous and volatile inanimate objects. Every prop, indeed, every character, is also a potential projectile. This basic premise still lies behind virtually every comedy

Hollywood now produces, from the food fights and panty raids of *Revenge of the Nerds* to the supernatural events of *Ernest Goes to Jail,* in which a janitor receives an electric shock of such high voltage that he becomes a human magnet and is chased around rooms by metal filing cabinets that stalk him wherever he goes, clashing together like cymbals as he narrowly escapes being flattened between them. The plots of such comedies are not stories in the conventional sense; they are austere and almost avant garde exercises in the cinematic application of aerodynamics and ballistics, the principles by which things spin and boomerang, veering off course and ricocheting into carefully arranged sets of obstacles. Each episode revolves around a nearly academic study of an instance of impact, collision, and rebound, the physics of speed and velocity that make this most popular form of low-brow comedy surprisingly abstract and cerebral, freed of the constraints of narrative.

It is because of this preoccupation with inanimacy that both the basic style of mass entertainment and the degree of its morbidity have changed dramatically during the last few decades as slapstick slowly acquired the jittering and hysterical quality of zaniness. The dehumanizing aesthetic that cinema borrows from ancient forms of popular entertainment, that is, its constant reduction of the bodies of its characters to mere things, is uniquely adapted to expressing our alienating involvement with the mechanized environment of consumerism and derives much of its current giddiness and wild, kinetic power from our interactions with gadgetry. As seen in the antics of such shrill comedians as Micky Rooney, Jerry Lewis, Lucille Ball, and Buddy Hackett, the innocuous acrobatics of venerable forms of mass culture found a fatal new source of inspiration in the malfunctioning of electrical equipment, a plot device that generated so many comic situations that it permanently relocated slapstick from Chaplin's poverty-stricken streets and bare, propless rooms to a baroque landscape of complex and intractable appliances. Slapstick became "zany" when it discovered contemporary home electronics, which drastically accelerated the pace of early types of cinematic humor and opened the floodgates to the endless holocaust of cars and appliances that is reenacted in so many current comedies in which the Machine Age self-destructs in our living rooms and kitchens.

The 1963 film *It's a Mad, Mad, Mad World,* a zany classic about a marathon race to find a bank robber's buried treasure, is a perfect example of what happened to silent comedy when it moved off of the sidewalks and onto the highways. The film is designed to showcase that most twentieth-century of consumer items, the automobile, which is the real hero of this wild goose chase, an inanimate protagonist that easily upstages the living characters who, despite their nerve-wracking performances, seem like lifeless props in comparison with the movie's convoys of speeding vehicles. In fact, in a genre that often amounts to little more than an homage to modern methods of locomotion, the automobile proves to be a far more effective comedian than the human being, able to withstand the rigors and physical duress of zaniness as it is tossed, crushed, flipped, and eventually ditched during films that portray a strange sacrificial ceremony consisting solely of gory hecatombs of Fords and Pontiacs, a rite of conspicuous destruction seemingly vital to our culture's mental health. The entire plot of National Lampoon's *Vacation,* for example, revolves around the methodical demolition of the family automobile during a summer trip, a ritual as resonant with anthropological significance as the dismemberment of fertility gods, especially in the scene in which the car becomes an open coffin for a cantankerous aunt, who, after dying from heat exhaustion, is covered in a tarpaulin and strapped to the roof. The film provides an excellent example of the principle of entropy that rules the zany cosmos, a world ravaged by the progressive disintegration of the baffling contraptions around which we arrange our entire lives.

Zaniness sensitized us to the potential for anarchy implicit in our ungovernable new possessions. As the destruction and misuse of property began to play a greater role in contemporary comedies, zaniness came to embody our dazed reaction to modernity, a kind of spaciness caused by our failure to keep abreast of the technological advances occurring around us. The result was the rise of the Hollywood ditz, a disoriented character who lurches from land mine to booby trap, victimized by accessories that constantly seem to be rising up in mutiny against him. Many of the zaniest episodes of *I Love Lucy* involved the antics of a woman portrayed as a perpetual hostage to labor-saving devices, a lovable imbecile marooned in a household of exploding blenders and wayward vacuum cleaners, of newfangled home accessories that imperiled the physical, as well as marital, well-being of a heroine treated as a cautionary figure, a tragically inept homemaker who fails to adapt to the modern environment. Flakiness thus became one of the crucial ingredients of zaniness, the bewildered state of incomprehension that lends the characters of contemporary comedies their distinctive air of muddled discomposure, the nuttiness that has infected the manner in which real people interact. This aura of absentmindedness, the cataleptic condition of post-traumatic stress syndrome exemplified by Lucy, is now copied verbatim off of the silver screen and adopted by ordinary men and women as a means of making each other laugh.

If consumerism gave zaniness its characteristic look, that of a battlefield of smoldering vehicles and vandalized suburban homes, rendered uninhabitable by the demolition derbies that American cinema wages within them, the rise of the counterculture in the 1950s and 1960s gave it its characteristic ideology. One of the most significant ways in which slapstick has evolved in the course of the twentieth century, from the drab collisions of bodies in *City Lights* to the orgies of destruction in such modern goofball films as *Police Squad* and *Loaded Weapon,* is that we have reinterpreted the zany hero's hyperactivity as an indication of his nonconformity and liberation, qualities absent from silent classics in which the hero was not a rebel but simply a buffoon, an absurd, if touching, court jester. When Charlie Chaplin and Buster Keaton played the roles of demented fugitives from justice, they were not enticing us with images of liberated revolutionaries on the loose, Thelmas and Louises who fly in the face of the status quo, the sort of cinematic radicals who now exploit their audience's post-countercultural fantasies of themselves as defiant oddballs, mavericks breaking out of social conventions. The misbehavior of John Belushi in *Animal House,* for example, was meant to convey his nihilistic freedom from propriety, an effect he achieved by performing obscene, Karen Finlayesque acts of food desecration at toga parties and in cafeterias, spewing out half-chewed donuts at the dinner table and dowsing his fellow students with the beer he constantly sprays on them like a spritzer bottle. One of the most seductive features of zaniness for the contemporary audience is the self-flattering vision it offers of disobedience, of the stubborn assertion of the self, in all of its unsocialized singularity, against the strictures of a society intolerant of individuality. This basic allegorical subtext lies behind such films as *Revenge of the Nerds,* in

which the social outcasts of an Ivy League campus—
four-eyed mama's boys, nose-picking slobs, and minc-
ing homosexuals—rise up against battalions of frat
jocks, in all their Aryan virility.

While zaniness may appear to be impulsive and exu-
berant, it in fact constitutes the most tribal, conformist,
and unspontaneous form of contemporary humor.
One of its major paradoxes is that, while it exalts disobedience on the screen, it systematically obliterates it
in the audience. The manufacturers of zaniness do not
sell comedy to us, they sell the opportunity for collective laughter. We are not buying the content of their
films, we are buying the myriad occasions these films afford for gathering together in the darkness of cav-
ernous cinemas where we participate in basically
mirthless laugh-a-thons, orgiastic rites of uncontrollable merriment that reverberate with the unspoken
blackmail of zaniness, the ultimatum to surrender to
the inane comedy of its characters' pranks and es-
capades. Zaniness is not a humor of the smile, of the
silent, introverted grin. It invariably involves an extroverted display of enjoyment, of the hoots and hollers
we make as we are swept up in its spirit of mass delirium. Such films as *Police Academy* and *Airplane* make us

laugh, not because they are genuinely funny, but simply because other people happen to be laughing and because we actively enjoy the solidarity of contributing our own voices to the pandemonium occurring around us, the racket we make to demonstrate our acquiescence to the punitive will of the group.

For this reason, zaniness is a psychologically compromised form of humor in that its impetus stems from the pleasure of conforming to the mindless glee of the obedient crowd, whose laughter becomes all the more uproarious the more it fears the ostracism that would result from being the sole dissenters in the audience, sitting alone in stony and impassive silence. The hysteria of zany films is in some sense a reflection of the hysteria of the viewer, who is desperate to pass the test that will allow him to gain entrance into this circle of initiates, this viciously intolerant community of partiers. And herein lies the hoax of the aesthetic: Comedies arranged around the apotheosis of the misfit can be viewed and enjoyed only under conditions that preclude the rebelliousness they glamorize. As the manufactured disobedience of an essentially obedient culture, zaniness fosters the illusion that it is a celebration of marginal groups, of rejects and freaks, when in fact the experience of watching it is full of anxiety about being relegated to the very margins it professes to venerate, of being ostracized because of that most individualistic of all crimes, the refusal to laugh. In this way, through controlled nonconformity, mainstream culture costumes itself as its opposite, as a crazy, offbeat culture, an illusion from which even the most conventional members of the status quo derive intense comfort.

THE FUTURISTIC

W | hy does the telephone no longer ring? The strident peals of archaic rotary telephones have been replaced by throbbing, high-pitched electronic bleeps that are no more effective and, for many people, far less pleasant than the familiar clamor of the old fashioned bell. Well into the 1980s, the ring of the telephone was produced by the physical vibrations of a hollow piece of metal struck rapidly by a small clapper, a sound that was as mechanically comprehensible as any other noise in our daily environments. The new ring, however, does not suggest a simple physical activity of thumping or pounding, the percussive racket of something banging against something else; it is an otherworldly trill that is completely unrecognizable. Every time the telephone rings we unconsciously ask ourselves "what is *that?*"—a question that Bell Atlantic and Sprint have deliberately left unanswered, thereby mystifying the operation of an old appliance through the subtle manipulation of a key aspect of its aesthetic.

It is not as if the function of the telephone has changed; it does not do more things, enable us to talk to more people at greater distances. And yet this new computer-generated sound suggests that the telephone is more "advanced" simply because its ring is different, a tonal adjustment that implies greater capacity. Manufacturers exploit our naive confusion of aesthetics with utility, instilling awe through gratuitous variations of form that deceive us into believing that the novel appearance of cars with three wheels and toasters that resemble speeding chrome bullets necessarily enhances performance and efficiency. The futuristic stands the modernist dictum of "form follows function" on its head: Form does not *follow* function, form *pretends* to follow function but is actually an aesthetic end in itself, a decorative feature that ostentatiously proposes itself as a useful one. Staplers that look ready for take off and hair blowers designed like Martian ray guns are now dressed in a kind of utilitarian drag, a high-tech costume that, while completely unnecessary to an appliance's operation, contributes to its intimidating aura as a state of the art invention. It is far easier, after all, to manipulate a product's incidental embellishments to create the impression of strength and durability than it is to make that stereo speaker shaped like a NASA space capsule intrinsically more powerful.

The futuristic creates its imagery through willful disobedience, an almost bratty, aesthetic misbehavior, rather than through a genuine spirit of inventiveness, of artistic prescience about the appearance of tomorrow. Tea kettles are round, so futuristic tea kettles are square; chairs have four legs, so futuristic chairs have three; houses are opaque cubes, so futuristic houses are transparent fish bowls; windows are rectangles that open from the bottom, so futuristic windows are portholes that open from the side. The futuristic is often an exercise in perversity, in sheer contrariness. It is not a new aesthetic so much as the denial of an old one. It does not involve a clairvoyant vision of tomorrow but rather an ever-clearer sense of the obsolescence of the past which, through a crotchety series of negations and disavowals, it seeks to cancel out by creating a world of torturously unnecessary aesthetic euphemisms in which a coffee cup is no longer a coffee cup but a menacing zirconium sphere and a door is no longer a door but a retractable aperture as complex as a camera's shutter. Guesswork about the future, oracular predictions about the shape of appliances to come, are all but irrelevant to the real purpose of the futuristic (and, ironically, of its opposite, quaintness): to document how far the present has superseded the past, whose ungainly inventions and decorative clichés serve as flattering foils to the ingenuity of our own LaserKaraoke players, accordion flashlights that can be twisted like pretzels, and electronic skateboards with digital readouts for mileage and speed. Impatience with yesterday is thus misconstrued as a presentiment of tomorrow.

THE INSIDES OF OUR MACHINES

The false aesthetics of utilitarianism play upon the consumer's ignorance, which has become a fallow breeding ground for superstitions, the legends that circulate among the ever-growing class of the technologically illiterate, whose misapprehensions about machines have inadvertent pictorial consequences, giving rise to the primary graphic conventions of the futuristic. If Greek myths are attempts to explain the mysteries of nature, the new myths of cyberspace are attempts to explain the mysteries of appliances, which have become so incomprehensible that they are now the principal fetishes of an animistic religion that takes us on a fantastic voyage through fiber optic cables, circuit boards, and electrostatic storage units. Cyberspace, like the ring of the telephone, is part of the computer's high-tech drag. The lush colors and Piranesian architectural forms of virtual reality are a rich source of futuristic iconography, which provides consumers with a concrete visual image of what lies inside their terminals: not tangled skeins of twisted wire, but the rickety scaffolding of precipitous staircases that end abruptly in space, cantilevered over bottomless voids, empty galleries of stone columns, and winding tunnels that narrow into impassable dead ends.

There is even a new type of science fiction that squires the viewer around the interiors of computers, which are laid out like the grid of a metropolis, with elevated superhighways that hurtle weightlessly through the air and gigantic satellite dishes that pivot frantically, emitting visible pulses of electricity. Such spatial metaphors are three-dimensional reifications of the consumer's ignorance, which has inspired a recurrent cinematic fantasy that explains the operation of motherboards and "ultra high speed Zero Wait 128K SRAM Cache[s]" through a familiar narrative: Our PCs are actually haunted by their own genius loci, malevolent autocrats holed up in our terminals in a silicon fortress built from transistors and microchips. The success of the 1982 movie *Tron,* in which a computer is dominated by the evil taskmaster of a "hard drive," spawned a whole school of films that turn the PC into a full-fledged parallel universe. In *Ghost in the Machine,* a psycho killer is sucked into a mainframe, from which he continues to prey upon nubile coeds, sneaking out of fuse boxes and electrocuting them as they prance about barefoot in a state of loose undress; in *Lawnmower Man,* a deranged messiah sets up his own cult in cyberspace, wooing the docile masses through the screens of their computers and indoctrinating them with such Christlike pronouncements as "I have become the chip!" We bridge the widening gap between the users of computers and their manufacturers with colorful folklore that explains the enigmas of our machines by means of old wives' tales about homunculi, tiny extraterrestrial elves who, like Santa's helpers, industriously move bits of information from one memory card to another.

Because of its essentially regressive nature, the futuristic is an aesthetic that recycles imagery from a number of readily available sources, a fact that explains the medieval taint of futuristic art, as in computer games in which warriors in rusty chain mail lunge at each other with javelins tipped with vaporizing laser beams or surf time warps to reclaim Arthur's sword, Excalibur, hijacked by a twenty-fifth-century churl who speaks in a pseudo-Shakespearean dialect. Inventing a new "ring" for the computer involves cannibalizing archaic narratives and styles.

When it is not borrowing from the romantic conventions of sword-and-sorcery novels, the futuristic draws heavily from the vocabulary of an equally dated look, the psychedelic, which forms the foundation of the whole appearance of cyberspace, with its radioactive colors and nervous, fluctuating Op-Art forms. The entrance to virtual reality, the moment when the cyber-tourist actually penetrates the terminal screen, is almost always represented through images of whirling vortices and darkly lit tunnels, down which the user slides at dizzying speeds on turbojet toboggans and plutonium powered mopeds. Stepping beyond the looking glass is an hallucinogenic experience that deliberately evokes the drug culture of the 1960s, bringing to mind mescaline and mushrooms, Carlos Castaneda and Lucy in the Sky with Diamonds. The Apollonian world of the machine is ironically represented through Dionysian references to the irrational and the subjective, to delirious trances that conflate the terminal with the subconscious. The result is a barrage of phantasmagoric conceits: transparent gondolas that float across moonlit skies spinning with galaxies; iridescent dolphins that dart in and out of Egyptian pyramids made of women's faces; and silver pigeons that flee sadistic toddlers with flickering terminals for heads. The very emblem of logic and restraint, the computer, becomes the locus of fantasy and imagination, an effect that both mirrors and heightens the user's sense of awe at this inexplicably powerful new appliance whose cinematic special effects are anything but utilitarian, suggesting quixotic, visionary capacities entirely unrelated to the pragmatic functions they actually perform.

Cyberspace often looks like black light posters of Jimmy Hendrix or album sleeves for the Jefferson Airplane and the Grateful Dead because acid-trip imagery was intimately linked to the adolescence of many software designers, who grew up during a period in which yellow submarines and dilated eyes with atomic mushroom clouds for pupils were associated with rebelliousness and individuality. Cyberspace has such an ornate aesthetic because its inventors see themselves as anarchic pioneers, pictorial misfits who have incorporated the fantasy of disobedience into the very look of our PCs, which capitalize on the chic of insubordination and transgressiveness, the truculent self-assertion so absent from the conformist corporate culture in which most computer engineers now work. The psychedelic iconography of virtual reality not only mimics the disorientation of hypnotic states and hence reflects our mystification at our appliances, but, by evoking the look of flower power and the counterculture, fosters the illusion in both the computer's inventors and its users that our engagement with this most pivotal of corporate appliances is somehow subversive, even traitorous to our employers, whose payroll has been infiltrated by legions of would-be hackers and online terrorists.

If the aesthetic of the mod induces vertigo with its kaleidoscopic imagery, another of the major motifs of cyberspace also manipulates appearances simply to perplex the user. The depths of our PCs are frequently represented through the image of the labyrinth, an endless maze of smoky hallways and perilous cul-de-sacs which open up at every turn as the cyber-tourist tears down blind corridors pursued by kamikaze "Dark Templars" and mutant "Zergs" ready to blast him into oblivion in a blaze of phaser fire. The Borgesian look of cyberspace is in part determined by computer action games and the chase plot, a narrative whose full dramatic potential is best realized in a minefield of obstructions in which doors slam shut in front of thermonuclear attack ships and spikes jut out of stone walls, impaling unwary escapees of interplanetary penal colonies. Jungles of narrow streets, tunnels, and dungeons are also designed to produce feelings of claustrophobia, of confinement, of being inside the box, held hostage in a twilight zone in which there is no outside world, no nature, no great open spaces, but only the oppressively close, tightly circumscribed realm of the indoors, the steamy hothouse of the biosphere or the cramped quarters of the deep-space probe.

In addition to intensifying the puerile thrills and chills of ambushes and dogfights and exaggerating the sensation of entrapment, of unventilated interiority, the labyrinth is an apt image of our inability to understand what really goes on inside circuit boards, which are so inscrutable that they have inspired the image of the maze, a gigantic obstacle course in which we crawl around like microscopic creatures through canyons of transistors, switches, and alkaline cells. The circuit board is a full-fledged architectural space in virtual reality, a nightmarish setting in which we wander down boulevards of electrodes and gleaming chips, which provide deadly arenas for countless battles for survival.

Cyberspace is also a world of high velocity and sudden change. Futuristic images rarely retain their shape for more than a few seconds before they metamorphose into something entirely different, their colors bleeding into each other, merging into blotches of sparkling pixels that immediately coalesce into new forms. Computer artists are so determined to display their virtuosity that they have created an entirely protean look for the futuristic, which is disconcertingly unstable, always ready for the next costume change, with a Day-Glo yellow fish swimming in a tropical aquarium changing into a bright blue chrysanthemum that waves its Technicolor petals at passing bumble bees, or wolves dallying amorously with sheep morphing into JFKs fondling Marilyn Monroes.

The software designer's exhibitionism, his irresistible longing to show off the gaudy potential of his powerful new programs, finds one of its most brilliant expressions in a recurrent pictorial theme of science fiction, the chimera made out of liquid mercury, one of the primary icons of the futuristic, as in Arnold Schwarzenegger's *Terminator II* in which a time-traveling villain assumes a menagerie of forms whose deadly plasticity can be thwarted only when he stumbles into a walk-in freezer and shatters into tiny splinters of silver ice. The high priority that the futuristic places on the visuals of constant change creates a world that is always evolving, always advancing, mutating, tyrannized by an aesthetic of uncontrollable malleability. Such an aesthetic embodies our belief in progress, our ebullient confidence that we are marching toward ever more perfect forms. The suppleness of the futuristic, its volatility and impermanence, are ideally suited to a consumerist society whose possessions are subject to habitual variation, to continual modifications of design that, however cosmetic, are intended to express both subtle improvements in function and startling augmentations of power.

The mysteries of such an unseen but pivotally important force as raw power kilowatts, volts, electric currents, magnetic fields, and radioactive emissions, are the very subject of the futuristic, whose images have been designed to give a physical presence to the energy that lights our rooms and cooks our meals. The appearance of science fiction in particular is dominated by an oddly demonstrative aesthetic that creates a tangible shape for that which eludes representation: for sound waves, which are drawn like concentric ripples emanating from radar stations and transmission towers; for radioactivity, which engulfs whole cities in clouds of sulfurous light; for magnetic fields, which draw spaceships to their ruin with glowing "tractor" beams; or for speed, which leaves ghostly streaks in space as the starship *Enterprise* accelerates full-throttle to warp nine. The futuristic is an homage to fuel, which it celebrates through a type of aesthetic theophany, the earthly manifestation of the God Energy, or, in the words of *Star Wars,* "The Force," a pulsing "field created by all living things," an immaterial savior that appears amongst us clothed in a familiar set of pictorial conventions.

The false aesthetics of utilitarianism, the attempt to give our appliances the equivalent of a new ring, frequently employ the metaphor of the macrocosm within the microcosm, the galaxy within the terminal whose screen is a trap door that opens onto infinity, as in an advertisement for JAZ 1GM storage drives, which "fit five Fortune 500 companies, a warehouse full of big ideas, and the entire kingdom of Valhalla into a four-inch square." Confusions of scale, juxtapositions of the infinitesimal with the infinite, a virus reproducing in a cell with a supernovae, an amoeba with a whale, suggest that advances in both microscopes and telescopes have inspired a bewilderingly relative iconography that inverts all sense of proportion, as in the Fijitsu commercial in which three of the company's top executives are shown skateboarding through cyberspace on gigantic microchips, precariously maintaining their balance in full suits and ties. Such visual paradoxes are crucial to the look of modern advertising and are the direct aesthetic consequence of the fact that companies are making ever-more-powerful machines with ever-greater memories in ever-smaller sizes, as in the case of so-called palm-top computers or the faddish new generation of "strap-ons," from computer belts and goggles with built-in PCs to class rings that contain crystals more powerful than the first Pentagon satellite. Miniaturization, the movement away from sprawling mainframes that once occupied entire city blocks toward portable, pocket-sized devices that are inconceivably faster than the unwieldy dinosaurs of the recent past, has led to a whole school of iconography that toys with nonsensical disparities of scale, with fetuses gestating inside planets, à la *2001: A Space Odyssey*, and nebulae exploding in the pupil of an eye, hurling molten boulders of primordial matter through a pitch-black void.

THE OUTSIDE OF OUR MACHINES

The futuristic is not a single, unified aesthetic but is fractured into two distinct components, the first pertaining to the voluptuously sensual, almost painterly images within the box and the second to the box itself. If our machines have a vivid internal life, they often have inexpressive and illegible exteriors, featureless black and beige facades stripped of the accretions of disfiguring parts, all of which are treated with an unaccountably shamefaced technological prudery and kept carefully out of sight. The aesthetic of our appliances is frequently conservative, monotonous, and subdued, not only because machines, in their unsensuousness and anonymity, clash with most styles of interior decoration and hence need to be disguised in an austere camouflage that allows them to blend inconspicuously with their surroundings, but because the act of hiding their internal mechanisms inside of spare, uncluttered cases increases their mysterious aura by stimulating curiosity about what lies within them.

The almost puritanical plainness of the external surfaces of our appliances is directly linked to the luxuriance of their internal mechanisms, the lush imagery of virtual reality, which offers opulent narratives instead of straightforward explanations, electronic fables instead of drearily matter-of-fact operational manuals. The monolithic aesthetic of the inscrutable cube, which is either entirely free of openings or equipped with one or two apertures with which the user engages in a cerebral form of interspecies sex, sliding into these acrylic orifices disks, CD-ROMs, and videotapes, is the principal force behind one of the basic plots of science fiction: the attempt to open the black box to examine its construction. Sci-fi films often revolve around an elaborate ritual of prying open the hood, of peaking inside, blasting off the manufacturer's protective packaging, and then rummaging around amidst the complex viscera of our machines. Our appliances are Pandora's boxes, and in the movies we become this scourge of mankind, drilling through tin cans that house millions of microscopic codes, algorithms, and "image orthicons." Destruction is a pedagogic device, an act of educational vandalism, an autopsy in which we disembowel robots and cockpit panels to penetrate the unforthcoming aesthetic of our television sets, stereo speakers, and laptop computers, which stubbornly refuse to disclose their secrets.

The inaccessible look of the monolith also reflects the streamlining movement of the 1930s and 1940s, when our culture's obsession with speed and new forms of transportation led industrial designers to create an aesthetic that suggested acceleration even among inanimate objects, an effect artists achieved by eliminating all external obstructions that caused "drag," that is, friction. In the heyday of this movement, the slippery forms and sleek, unbroken contours of streamlined products became so routine that even coffins were streamlined, built like supersonic projectiles: torpedoes or bullets whose aerodynamic shapes determined the design of everything from irons to egg beaters, all of which appeared to be frozen in flight, as mercurial as a Brancusi sculpture. In the course of the twentieth century, the automobile has gone from being a clunky compilation of fenders, crank shafts, bumpers, bulb horns, radiator caps, and bug-eyed headlights to a smooth biomorphic shape in which all sharp corners have been eroded, all obtrusive parts pushed inwards, hidden under a body-hugging enamel shell. The grills are gone, the bumpers have disappeared, the fenders have grown into the frame and the boxy cab into the hood, creating an Arp-like sculpture of subtle depressions and imperceptible convexities that turn the machine into a living structure, not a slapdash assemblage of independent components.

The startling contrast between the inside and the outside of our machines mystifies the process of their assembly, making it seem as if our appliances had assembled themselves, grown in one piece like real organisms, an effect made possible by the development of materials that enable manufacturers to produce the bodies of our cars and television sets in ever-larger sections rather than cobbling them together from innumerable small parts. The futuristic abhors the seam, its Achilles' heel, which offers incriminating evidence of welding, nailing, and gluing, the tell-tale signs of the grease-spattered mechanic whose handiwork belies its pretenses of autonomy and omnipotence. Industrial designers take great pains to conceal joints and rivets to obscure the process of assembly and promote the myth that our appliances were, not built, so much as born in a mysterious process of spontaneous generation that contributes to their intrigue, much as the narratives of cyberspace falsify the operation of computers.

For all of their ostensible usefulness, the aesthetics of utilitarianism are remarkably impractical and are often met with stiff resistance. The characterless appearance of our appliances is the result of what Raymond Loewy, one of the founding fathers of the streamlining movement, identified as the MAYA principle ("most advanced yet acceptable"), a basic rule of industrial design intended to accommodate the consumer's skittishness, to placate his need for continuity and his distrust of change. History is littered with dazzlingly original, futuristic duds (Buckminster Fuller's car with three wheels, to name just one), which, while they may be admired as academic curiosities, are too intimidating, too freakishly unfamiliar, to compete with conservative, tried-and-true brand names, whose unoriginal shapes inspire confidence in their strength and reliability. One of the disappointing consequences of the

MAYA principle is the growth of an aesthetic status quo that makes our domestic environments prosaic and unimaginative, with every Maytag identical to every Westinghouse, every Whirlpool to every Speed Queen, all of which scrupulously adhere to what was once called "the survival form," the Platonic prototype of the ideal Middle-American freezer and washing machine.

It is in part because of this strong psychological need for uniformity, coupled with our impatience with a world in which every refrigerator and oven looks exactly alike, that science fiction continues to fascinate us, presenting a world in which the MAYA principle has given way to an unbridled celebration of extravagant forms, of spheroid chairs, tubular coffee makers, saucer-shaped computers, and triangular cars. But it is not only science fiction that desecrates MAYA and smashes the mold of the "survival form," but its real-life equivalents, NASA and the defense industry, which, because they both manufacture and purchase their own products, are immune to market forces and hence can be as experimental as they choose. The very bastion of reactionary politics, the military, is thus ironically an aesthetic standard-bearer in the field of design and an inspiration for the futuristic, from radar-evading

Stealth bombers to Telstar communications satellites, from Trident nuclear submarines to Thor Delta ballistic missiles. When teenage boys settle in for an evening of mayhem playing their favorite computer game, nuking "marauding metallic battalions of mechanized death machines," they are not just giving in to their raging hormones but, like the most fastidious of connoisseurs, are appreciating the appearance of a world liberated from the tedium of MAYA, exploring possibilities of design and color that a conservative economy has suppressed, preferring instead the security of cautious visual tautologies. These destructive pubescent vandals are actually aesthetes in disguise who, while admittedly intoxicated by the power of reducing the Mutalisks' Valkyrie Missile Frigates to scrap metal, are also captivated by the sensual qualities of their games' "stunning graphics," "amazing lighting effects," and "intricately modeled environments."

The loss of control we have experienced over our unchanging, monolithic appliances has led manufacturers to devise false methods of instilling in the user feelings of complete control, of macho, chest-thumping intellectual brawn, the virile mastery of the online Rambo. No sooner do the players of the computer game Quake loosen their ties and enter the cockpits of their attack ships than they metamorphose from mild-mannered office workers into "badass, bomb-lobbing bull[ies] who love . . . to spill blood and roll heads." The futuristic conflates the aesthetic of two machines, the PC and the car, creating a strange mechanical amalgam, the computer-mobile, an unruly mythical beast whose keyboard is a steering wheel, its terminal a windshield, its joy stick a gear shaft, and its CPU a race car or even a bucking bronco at an electronic rodeo, as in an ad for the Internet search engine WebRecord that reads "chase it, rope it, hog-tie it and print it. Yee-Haw! You're the big bad Web wrangler." Fantasies of subduing our machines through hand-to-hand combat, tackling them to the ground and forcing them to do our bidding, have become ever more important as our appliances have become more automated, running themselves with almost no human intervention whatsoever.

The evolution of the aesthetic of the control panel in both real life and in science fiction reflects the decline of brute strength in the use of our machines, which don't need to be pedaled, pumped, and stoked with coal but can unleash floods, destroy whole skyscrapers, snarl traffic to a gridlocked standstill, and obliterate hostile nations with the slightest touch of a tiny button. Earlier in the twentieth century, the control panels on everything from radios and hand-cranked victrolas to flying saucers and Robby the Robot's built-in coffee dispenser featured dials that had to be twisted, levers that had to be pulled, toggle switches that had to be flipped, and circuit breakers that had to be thrown. The contemporary control panel, however, can be operated by merely tapping a flashing icon on a terminal screen, as in the case of our ATMs, a change that represents a small yet significant diminution of the role of our bodies in controlling our machines. What's more, the aesthetics of buttons themselves have changed in such a way that our physical involvement with them has decreased even further, the hard, metallic key giving way to a soft, fleshy cushion of rubber or a clickless heat sensor that can be activated simply by passing one's finger within centimeters of its surface or even blowing on it. Such changes in the sensuous experience of the whole act of button pushing have reconfigured our interactions with machines and contributed even further to our sense of passivity and our awe at our appliances' omnipotence.

The disappearance of the body from work is responsible for the unmitigatedly macho aesthetic of the futuristic, which compensates for the emasculation of deskbound office workers through militaristic fantasies in which the cyberspace alter egos of effete businessmen, the ballooning steroid monsters of virtual reality, are thrown into situations that involve amazing feats of agility and strength. Science fiction is suffused with what might be called machine envy, the desire to become our appliances, to incorporate them into our bodies, as in countless films in which hair-trigger, semi-automatic rifles and hydrogen rocket launchers have been grafted onto the hands of bionic hybrids who are little more than jigsaw puzzles of prosthetic parts, with infrared implants for eyes and memories enhanced with silicon chips embedded in the cerebral cortex.

The hyper-masculine look of the futuristic and its elimination of every trace of femininity can be seen in the explosive conflicts that arise over an elementary device that science fiction often eliminates: the door knob, a homely piece of low-tech hardware that has become what is now fashionably called a "site" in which we triumph over our humiliated sense of redundancy in an automated world. We do not open doors in futuristic dwellings and spacecraft, they spring open by their own volition with a pneumatic whoosh, lifting magically before us as we stride from cabin to cabin, tripping light beams that cause spiral panels to retract. Ironically, however, the absent door-knob plot is consoling to our wounded sense of physical esteem because the high-tech door almost never works but jams at the very moment that the decontamination procedures that will blow the space station to smithereens have been activated and an inappropriately saccharine, computer-generated voice murmurs "access denied" as warning sirens blare and cyanide gas begins to seep through the vents of the air-circulation system. We do not turn handles and calmly step over thresholds in sci-fi films; we blast our way through futuristic doors, slamming our shoulders against them, knocking them down with battering rams, blowing them off their hinges, or zapping them with fusillades of laser beams. The plots of sci-fi films and their obstreperously macho aesthetic often focus on the return of the body, of the need for brawn, for brute strength, the human hand, which triumphs over brainy electronic wizardry in a narrative whose action is based on a process of devolution, from the high tech to the low tech, from the malfunctioning microchip to the bulging bicep. The sedentary nature of the lives we lead in offices thus plays a key role in the fantasies that lie at the basis of the rugged look of the futuristic, which allays our fears of displacement by machines and counteracts our presumed feminization by transforming us into camouflage-fatigued commandos who wage war deep within the trenches of our PCs.

DELICIOUSNESS

S tart off with our thick 'n crispy home style French fries or our tangy Buffalo wings pan-seared to seal in the wholesome goodness and brought to your table on a sizzling platter of seasonal vegetables swimming in a savory, full-flavored wine sauce teeming with a generous medley of herbs and spices. Or try a bowl of our signature soup du jour or our garden-fresh house salad with five scrumptious veggies topped with the crunchiest of homemade croutons and smothered in chunky, made-from-scratch *bleu* cheese dressing. Then sink your teeth into our Colossal Fish Sandwich drizzled with zesty Creole-style mustard and served on a deluxe golden-brown bakery bun accompanied with a hearty portion of—olé!—authentic corn-fresh tortilla chips drenched in real melted

American cheese. Or savor the succulent juiciness of our legendary Baby Back Ribs, a full slab of plump, mouth-watering Danish pork ribs lightly brushed with country-style barbecue sauce, grilled to perfection, and then nestled on a bed of char-broiled onions.

The rhetoric with which advertisers make love to our tastebuds often has nothing whatsoever to do with how our Cajun McChicken Sandwiches, Taco Bell Meximelts, Eskimo Pies, and Rice-a-Roni San Francisco treats really taste but constitutes a highly fictional fantasy about how processed foods *should* taste in a utopian world in which imaginary farmers, rising at the crack of dawn, harvest everything from their own fields, picking the tomatoes fresh from the vine, their boots caked with manure. The misrepresentations of the aesthetic of deliciousness must be understood as part of a systematic campaign, not only on the part of chain restaurants but of food manufacturers in general, to camouflage the insipidity of packaged goods and neutralize the skepticism of a society still adjusting to its loss of control over all aspects of food production. While delighted by the convenience of "He-Man Hot Dish[es]" that are "sliced 'n diced 'n handy," we are nonetheless alarmed at the menace of potentially unwholesome foods injected with toxic dyes, sprayed with defoliating insecticides, and steeped in carcinogenic preservatives. So much of what we think of as delicious is not a description of the way food has tasted throughout history, whether it was prepared in the kitchen of a pharaoh or a pope, on the campfire of a caveman or the electric coils of a self-cleaning Magic Chef oven, but the way it has tasted for only the last 150 years. With calculated exuberance, McDonald's, Kellogg's, and Pillsbury put a healthy spin on the commercialization of the kitchen, wooing wary housewives with an extremely stylized language that allays qualms about the nutritional vacuity of meals so simple to prepare that all you have to do is "sit home and chew."

That deliciousness is an historically specific invention of the twentieth century in response to the inadequacies of instant foods becomes particularly clear in the repetition of the word "freshness" in advertisements for everything from Cheddar Cheese Goldfish ("hand-delivered fresh to stores everyday") to the Jolly Green Giant's Niblets ("fresh from the can means fresh from the fields because they are packed when dewy fresh"). "Freshness" becomes an attribute of flavor only when food goes stale on store shelves, moldering in warehouses, languishing in crates in over-heated cargo holds, and housewives begin to depend on factories for even the most perishable of items, like breads and pastries, which harden within hours, or milk, which curdles overnight. Whereas "freshness" was once taken for granted because food was no sooner harvested than eaten, it has become nothing less than a cultural fetish in an era in which the interval between the packaging of a product and its actual consumption has been prolonged for months or even years by the miracles of refrigeration, chemical preservatives, freeze-drying, irradiation, the dehydration of vegetables, and even Tupperware. Similarly, words like "crunchy," "crispy," and "moist" actually mean "not soggy," "not stale," and "not desiccated," problems that pertain not to the intrinsic taste of food but to what happens to flavor in aluminum cans, plastic bags, and Mylar pouches, containers in which our Babe Ruths and Dipsey Doodle Corn Chips dry out, lose texture, or are pulverized into heaps of broken crumbs. When our foods lose their crunch, when they turn into mealy pulp on the shelves of the neighborhood bodega, when they shrivel up into sapless husks in frozen food lockers, when they are squashed flat as pancakes on lurching eighteen-wheelers, we begin to value the very qualities most endangered by the vagaries of transport and packaging and to describe flavor in terms of a product's ability to survive the grueling pilgrimage from the cattle ranch and the orchard to the dining room table. Deliciousness, in short, is not actually delicious but is closely related to its opposite, to the nauseous, the inedible, the unappetizing, to the fact that the crunchy golden crusts of that zesty frozen pizza are as jaw-breakingly tough as shoe leather, that that lusciously moist, heavenly rich, melt-in-your-mouth instant chocolate cake is so dry that choking children clutch their parched throats and cry out for milk, and that those "downright habit-forming" all-natural crispy corn curls are so brittle that they shatter into salty granules of flour and monosodium glutamate.

The subtext of nausea behind deliciousness is also apparent in another aspect of flavor specific to consumerized foods—chunkiness, a word that combats two separate problems that have arisen in the age of canned goods: the tendency of manufacturers to cut corners on cost and skimp on ingredients; and, more important, the consumer's distrust of food that has been poached and blenderized beyond recognition, liquefied into a molten puree in industrial steam cookers. Our loss of control as cooks and our ignorance of what really went into that glowing orange cheese substitute in the convenient squeeze tube, those arterially red Spaghetti-Os, and that geometrically perfect wedge of Spam, have led to a backlash against a type of food that is nothing more than a cocktail of chemicals, one we increasingly refuse to swallow unless manufacturers itemize its contents. The result of this distrust is what might be called a new food extroversion, a studied display of ingredients, of whole pecans, recognizable "chunks" of tomatoes, florets of broccoli, spears of asparagus: the visible evidence of real foods that reassures the consumer that he is eating an identifiable substance and not some tainted mystery meat concocted from chicken offal and horse giblets. Just as lengthy delays between harvesting and consumption produce "freshness" and desiccation on store shelves produces "moistness," so another problem caused by consumerism produces "chunkiness," the fear of both contaminants and the mysteries of the homogenized merchandise we purchase in the Safeway.

The need to know what a product is made of, to crack the code of the top secret industrial recipe, has also led to a new form of externalized food photography in which nothing is hidden: The vegetables of soups float

weightlessly on the surface of the bowl rather than sinking to the bottom (a trick performed with naturally buoy-
ant dehydrated products and, in some cases, with a
subaqueous pyramid of transparent marbles); opaque
sauces are placed *around* a dish rather than dribbling
down its sides, thus hiding it from view; and the flakes of
breakfast cereals stand rigidly upright like gravestones,
defying gravity, proudly displaying their crispiness and
crunch, securely anchored in a sturdy, milk-like foundation of sour cream mixed with Elmer's Glue. Even a
frontal photograph of something as straightforward as a
club sandwich is now really just a sculptural inventory of
ingredients, a dexterous, trompe l'oeil feat in which
each tier is slightly recessed from the one beneath it,
arranged like a staircase and propped up from behind by
a complex scaffolding of clamps and toothpicks that en-
sures that the contents of each stratum can be examined.

Deliciousness was once a fiercely modernist aesthetic
that celebrated the technological inventions that liberated the housewife from the kitchen. Unlike contemporary food advertisements, which are oddly reticent
about describing the electric churns, hydraulic
blenders, and computerized pressure cookers in which
food is now prepared, advertisements from the early

part of the century showcased the futuristic conveniences of modern equipment, as in the case of the "Scientific Foods" of "Professor Anderson," a culinary alchemist who, in the late nineteenth century, created Quaker Oats's Puffed Wheat and Puffed Rice by "blasting the starch granules to pieces [in] an explosion of steam." An advertisement from 1910 expresses the amazement the consumer felt at Anderson's transformation of the kitchen into a state-of-the-art industrial refinery when it tells us that "these are foods shot from guns, and this is the curious process. The whole wheat or rice grains are put into sealed guns. Then the guns are revolved for sixty minutes at 550 degrees. . . . Every starch granule is so blasted to pieces that the digestive juices act instantly." The modernist love of artificial food "ideas" and "concepts," as they were once called, can also be seen in the psychedelic palette of food advertisements from the 1950s and 1960s, which revel in the lurid novelty of the machine-made look, in the bright colors of canned strawberries covered in a bright membrane of crimson syrup, rosy tuna fish salad resting on a jiggling slab of lime green jello, and bloody slices of canned tomato smeared with dollops of cottage cheese and topped with limp strips of dyed pimento.

Well into the 1970s and 1980s, the technological in-genuity of packaged foods was so integral to their ap-peal that deliciousness was often not about food at all but about containers, about the miracle of the can, about the packaging revolution that created the need for the aesthetic of deliciousness in the first place. Food advertisements from the first half of the century often consisted of blown-up images of the can itself sur-rounded by a spiky nimbus of light that illuminated the ecstatic faces of shopping housewives and their adoring offspring, who threw their hands into the air, making idolatrous gestures, as if they were witnessing a theo-phany, the appearance of the Messiah in aisle five. Just as computer manufacturers foster superstitious rever-ence for our PCs by turning the terminal into a micro-cosm of the universe, a black box that contains spinning galaxies and clusters of exploding stars, so food manu-facturers instilled reverence for the can by portraying it as a magical device capable of trapping actual physical samples of fragrant breezes, spring showers, morning dew drops, and the mellow rays of the Mediterranean sun. The can was once a microcosm that contained the macrocosm, an Aladdin's Lamp that bottled up a genie of flavor so evanescent that it had to be captured fresh

161

from the vine, rushed to the processing plant, placed in a container, and then released with a whoosh of the vacuum seal to do the housewife's bidding. Because canned foods liberated our diets from both the seasons and geography, giving pineapples to the Eskimos and peaches to New Yorkers snowbound in the arctic winter months, the can was indeed "one of the real miracles of our twentieth century life," as Libby proudly proclaimed in 1921. Andy Warhol was right to pay homage to its image, for it exerts the same effect on the kitchen as television exerts on culture, leveling regional cuisine, internationalizing food, and producing a kind of dietary Esperanto in regions once dependent on the meats and vegetables of local farmers.

The cult of the container no longer has the same zealous following as it did in the 1920s, when DelMonte sang the praises of "the can that makes Summer last all year long," but is now the object of shame, the archenemy of flavor, the nemesis of our taste buds and not a supernatural contraption that brings the tropics to our doorstep, moving coconut groves and coffee plantations into our kitchen cabinets. Food advertisements for the most part now guiltily avoid images of packages (if they are represented at all, they are usually consigned to a far corner of the page) and focus instead on ostensibly homemade food that is displayed on tables gleaming with crystal, illuminated with candles, and groaning with a wide array of gourmet delicacies. This startling change from tin to fine china testifies to our increasing technophobia, our discomfort with the invasion of the laboratory into the kitchen. Once a modernist aesthetic, deliciousness is now virulently anti-modernist, full of disgust for the "husband-dazzling" instant tapiocas and the "whoppingly wonderful" fruit cocktails of the 1950s, the unabashed Frankensteins of food science, chock full of carcinogenic additives, acid pink dyes, and irradiated vegetables.

Our growing dislike of the processed look has produced another key feature of the aesthetic of deliciousness: "texture," a reaction against foods so emulsified that they are entirely texture*less*, as bland and homogenized as Crisco, Philadelphia Cream Cheese, or Blue Bonnet Margarine, whose lumpless uniformity is the result of the "107 steel fingers [that] do the blending." Technophobia has triggered a sudden renaissance in imperfections: in crunchy old-fashioned peanut butter in contrast to the "creamy" comestibility of Jiffy, water-repellent cereals with honey-glazed clusters of granola in contrast to the sugary slush of macerated corn flakes, and whole-wheat bread with cracks and craters in contrast to the flawless, slide-rule perfection of an undeviatingly flat slice of Wonder. While we at first welcomed the amelioration of the miserable lot of the oppressed housewife slaving over the hot coals of her potbellied stove, our fear of machines makes us long to put her back in her place, to restore the cook to the kitchen, to create evidence of the human touch, of chopping, hacking, dicing, slicing, and carving. These studied irregularities are in themselves highly artificial and machine-made, meant to suggest the ragged unevenness of a mythic homemaker whose unsteady, trembling hand constantly slips, misses, and miscalculates. If quaintness creates artificial discolorations and scratches in brand new things, gouging the surfaces of new chairs with chisels and ice picks so that they will absorb the "character" of their owners, deliciousness also creates "character" through a form of food mutilation, through "texture." Just as quaintness rebels against the tyranny of the new by sabotaging soulless commodities and avoiding plastics, Formicas, and stainless steels, so deliciousness turns processed foods into made-from-scratch entrees by manufacturing defects that attest to the trauma of a product's preparation. Software designers help us overcome the alienating sterility of computers by building into their programs small, humorous reminders of a whimsical human intelligence—the cackling laughter of an error message, for instance, or the sophomoric wisecracks of mildly salacious screen savers, seemingly unnecessary details that transform the PC from a heartless automaton into a teasingly playful type of folk art. The alienating sterility of processed foods has given rise to a similar need for the human touch, creating a type of *edible* folk art.

Food manufacturers take the metaphor of folk art at face value in their efforts to portray themselves as the uncompromising enemies of mass production. The eerie, sci-fi image of those 107 spinning steel fingers has led to a type of rhetoric that transforms each Milky Way candy bar, Little Debbie Cupcake, and individually wrapped Kraft Single into an exquisite treasure, every granule of which has been carefully prepared and inspected by an army of quality control experts who, in white gloves and laboratory smocks, pore over the entire harvest, conscientiously "selecting" every coffee bean, potato, and kernel of corn. Food advertisers re-

165

store the missing cook to the kitchen by taking an obsessively molecular view of their products, which they insist have been so thoroughly micro-managed that "every chip," "every flake," "every drop," "every sip," "every bite," and "every crunch" is the outcome of calculated premeditation. In this way, the bustling assembly line becomes a cozy country kitchen presided over, not by a line of sullen butchers who pluck fistfuls of feathers off the carcasses of dead chickens and splatter their entrails on the floor, but by a traditional housewife in a tidy apron who serves her family only the daintiest morsels that she herself has chosen according to the most exacting standards.

The rhetoric of anti-mass production also crops up in a recurrent set of words that invent a level of grammatical comparison beyond the superlative, as in "super supreme gourmet coffee," "arch deluxe French Fries," "off-the-chart delicious frozen fish sticks," "the creamiest of the crème de la crème cupcakes," "the pepperoniest pizza," "the most exceptionally unique seafood snack," and "the most 'utterly utter' apple butter"—expressions that exaggerate the singularity of a product, elevating it into a special category far above the characterless, generic goods sold to the public by impersonal conglomerates. Another grammatical distortion of deliciousness is the profusion of enigmatic comparatives which, without explanation, offer oblique allusions to the merchandise of unidentified competitors whose presence is constantly emerging in words like "fresher," "meatier," "heartier," "creamier," "toastier," "zestier," "richer," and "munchier," all of which raise the unanswered question, "fresher (and so on) than what?" Deliciousness, itself an aesthetic of consumerism, fashions itself as anti-consumerist and constantly nags and scolds about the perils of mass production, warning consumers about people who treat their cows with bovine growth hormones and prepare their products in unsanitary conditions, cooking hamburger patties tainted with E. coli and mixing ingredients in vats teeming with Salmonella. Food manufacturers impersonate committed consumer protectionists. They set themselves up as the Real McCoy in a system overwhelmed by frauds who squabble over market share even as the scrupulously honest makers of "real-milk milk shakes," "genuine chili dogs," "authentic cheddar cheese spreads," and "honest-to-goodness homemade potato chips" go quietly about the business of making quality foods. Consumerism is

167

constantly blackening its own eyes, disassociating itself from its own abuses, railing against the evils of mass production, and denigrating the competition.

The aesthetic of deliciousness can be best understood in relation to a major predicament that confronts all food manufacturers: Taste is the most indescribable of all sensory experiences and is therefore usually evoked in three unsatisfactory ways: through vague generalities ("deep-down deliciousness," "the zesty 'zip' that's making these hot new chips so popular"); categoric admissions of the failure of language to describe this elusive sensation ("inexpressibly divine," "unutterably good," "like nothing I have ever tasted"); or synesthetic comparisons that turn the mouth into a miniature concert hall where virtuosos like the Frito Bandito, Ronald McDonald, and Tony the Tiger perform "a symphony of sumptuous flavors," "a liquid lullaby," "a fugue of fantastic fudge tastes," and "a quartet of sauces." Because of the limitations of the media in depicting something that cannot be seen with the naked eye; taste, touch, and smell can be conveyed only through metaphors based on the other two senses, which lend themselves to representation on television and radio, whereas it is virtually impossible to make a football fan watching the Superbowl on a sofa thousands of miles from a studio in Burbank experience something as subjective and untranslatable as the flavor of a peach, the texture of a squeezably soft roll of toilet paper, or the smell of a perfume (although strides have been made in representing the latter through the scratch-and-sniff terrorism of such perfumers as Estee Lauder and Calvin Klein, who include samples of their products in women's magazines).

To help us visualize deliciousness, food advertisers adopt the same techniques as pornographers. They bring our faces as close to the food as possible, thus mimicking filmmakers, who naively believe that, by taking an obsessively nearsighted approach to intercourse and positioning the lens of the camera within centimeters of flickering tongues and thrusting pelvises, they are actually ushering the audience right into the scene and triggering the same excitement that the actors are feeling. Food manufacturers rub our faces in their products, shoving our noses flush against Mars Bars that break hypnotically in slow motion, their caramel centers stretching into translucent filaments; cataracts of diet soft drinks that cascade into frosty glasses, spitting a carbonated mist of thirst-quenching spray; and succulent Sunkist oranges that explode with one ravenous chomp, spewing jets of nectar in the equivalent of the stag film's "money shot."

To give us intimate access to the porn star's central nervous system, directors often insist that their performers engage in dirty talk, providing a running commentary on each sex act, as if they were witnessing the events rather than participating in them, declaring that "oh that feels so good," "yeah, you like that," and "this is hot." These oddly superfluous glosses on every bump and grind create an unnaturally extroverted form of lovemaking in which the actor functions as his own anchorman, his own MC, a loquacious expositor of his own arousal. To deal with the problems involved in selling taste, food advertisers also talk dirty to the consumer. They have invented an overly demonstrative style of eating in which people chew with their mouths open, smacking their lips as they savor the "long, lingering kiss of onion" in a fat-free salad dressing or "go cuckoo for Cocoa Puffs." In magazine advertisements and television commercials, the mouth becomes a detonation chamber in which foods "explode," "burst," and "erupt with flavor," and jaws become mandibles that feast on "Crunchopolis," "the loudest snack in the free world," or Munchie Nuggets, which are funneled down the hatch of a voracious cartoon kid who gulps and swallows with deafening gusto. Manufacturers pruriently invoke the moment of ingestion, as in a commercial for Very Fine Juices in which the rhythmic sounds of people licking their chops and slurping are set to music, or in an advertisement for Oreos that describes "two crisp chocolate cookies (m-m-mmm!) between which is velvety snow-white cream (ah-h-h!)." Much as the talkative porn star invents for the viewer a vicarious penis with his incessant commentary, so the food pornographer invents a vicarious tongue by feigning a presumably infectious delirium that entirely misrepresents our physical responses to flavor.

One curious thing is missing from advertisements that describe eating as a gastronomic orgy in which people devour anything they can lay their hands on, wolfing down whole boxes of Trix, packages of Little Debbie Apple Delights, and bags of Chester Cheeta's Cheetos—hunger. Food manufacturers almost never describe eating as a response to an animal need but instead pretend that Frito Lay's Au Gratin Chips and Guiltless Gourmet Nachos satisfy the fastidious craving of a connoisseur, who, far from being doubled over in pain, maintains his self-possession and powers of judgment even when he is famished. Consumerism conceals some of the physiological realities of eating (while exaggerating others) because hunger would degrade the product being sold, which must be "selected" for its putatively unique qualities and not for its unglamorous utility as fodder for growling stomachs that can't tell the difference between pâté de foie gras and Spam. In food advertisements, the tongue and not the belly is the focus of the appeal. To emphasize a product's unparalleled excellence, manufacturers ironically cannot talk about the very thing they strive so hard to elicit in their market: the urgent, biological needs of the bottomless maw, which must be ignored, more or less as if a pornographer were forced to describe sex without mentioning lust.

The spiritualizing of hunger, the attempt to recharacterize it as an aesthetic need rather than a biological one, leads food advertisers to describe their products as if they were priceless jewels and invaluable art works, like the First Colony Coffee's ad that shows a woman wearing a glittering diadem bedizened, not with gems, but with coffee beans above a caption that reads "precious enough to store in your vault or safe-deposit box,"

or the Grand Marnier Liqueur ad that shows an unfinished sculpture of the bottle, still trapped in its block of
marble, surrounded by a recently chiseled pile of stone
rubble. In the course of the twentieth century, the aesthetic of deliciousness has become so visual, so centered
on the eyes rather than on the tastebuds, that food photography has developed into a full-fledged art form
practiced by a painterly school of epicureans who freely
plagiarize the still lifes of Claesz and de Heem, setting
up splendid banquets with silver platters, porcelain
tureens, and exotic fruit, everything except the vanitas
motifs—the tell-tale fly, time piece, and death's head.

The mouth-watering pleasures of art desecration are
essential to the aesthetic of deliciousness, which turns
dishes into edible sculptures that we are encouraged to
vandalize, mauling such labor-intensive food follies as
bûches de Noel encrusted with meringue mushrooms,
dolmades meticulously tied with ribbons of leek strips,
and artificial flowers made out of fans of sliced
gherkins and tomatoes cut in spirals. Ostentatious photographs of dill fritattas, fromage blanc blinis, and baby
eggplant boats filled with Tunisian zucchini puree have
the same psychological effect on the consumer as
Tibetan sand paintings, whose beauty inheres in their

fragility and impermanence, in the invitation they offer to destroy their intricate patterns with one capricious swipe of the hand or kick of the foot. The transformation of food into art and art, in turn, into shit provides a subtle way of flattering the consumer, whom manufacturers implicitly portray as a refined cannibal, an "aesthetophage" who dines on paintings and sculptures, sending masterpieces on an inglorious journey down his alimentary canal. The degradation of expensive substances heightens our sense of self-importance as mythological kings and queens who are allowed to consign museum pieces to the most vulgar places in our bodies, where they are dissolved by salivary enzymes and gastric secretions.

As cooks spend less and less time in the kitchen, they engage in a brand new type of vicarious cooking by flipping through the pages of such glossy magazines as *Bon Appetit* and *Gourmet*, whose gorgeous images of "meltingly tender lamb [that] falls into a cardamom-accented coconut-milk sauce," "uplifting spinach enchilada[s]" "baptized in a fiery Jamaican marinade," and Kangaroo Fillet swimming in "truffle-infused *jus*" bear no relation whatsoever to contemporary culinary practices. In fact, these idealized images of perfect food bear an *inverse* relation to what we really eat. The less cooking we do and the more we rely on products like Rich's Southern Barbeque Frozen Sandwiches, whose preparation, according to a folksy belle in a polyester waitress uniform, involves "diddlysquat," the more we fantasize about an imaginary utopia where elaborate cooking still happens, where *nothing* comes out of a can, where *everything* is made from scratch, where we jealously supervise all stages of food preparation, squandering our time scouring grocery stores for rare spices and oriental vegetables obtainable only in remote shops in Chinatown. There is no more tangible evidence of our discontent with the decline of cooking than the rise of these new vehicles for food fantasizing, these dietary Harlequin romances that rejuvenate the jaded palate with lavish spreads of "quince sambal that perfectly partners the crisp and juicy bird" and "ethereal green lasagne" that "dances with the flavors of tamarind [and] mango." The death of real cooking stimulates the aesthetic of deliciousness, which is now centered not in our mouths but in our imaginations, in the extravagant visuals of both food photography and cooking shows, which provide pornography for the tastebuds, a form of surrogate eating for a dietetic age, one that no longer has the time to feed itself and that therefore must satisfy its frustrated appetites by admiring these mythic, nouvelle cuisine chimeras. The aesthetic of deliciousness is now entirely divorced from the sensation of taste and is rooted instead in pretty pictures, in looking rather than eating, in the optic nerve, the organ most amenable to advertising.

The equation of beauty and taste is a false one, however, for nothing ever tastes as good as it looks in food magazines. In fact, it is widely known that the food fantasies in *Gourmet* and *Bon Appetit* are actually inedible, that the voluptuous centerfolds of these gastronomical *Playboys* and *Penthouses* have communicable diseases, that that poulette "abetted by a mushroom velouté and lemon juice," those "willowy won ton strips gracing the salad," and those "bright vegetables buttressing the fish" are the equivalent of prosthetic food, potentially toxic concoctions of Super Glue and varnish, hair spray and shoe polish. Professional food photographers complain that the sets of shoots often reek with the fetid aroma of raw meats that have been seared only on the outside with paint strippers, blow torches, and acetylene welders, which cauterize the surfaces of slabs of beef and uncooked drumsticks, although they do tend to create crevices in T-bone steaks, which must be glued back together with liquid cement. Ice cream is made of Crisco and confectioners sugar so that it won't melt, the sesame seeds on hamburger buns have been sprayed on with spritzers of epoxy to achieve perfectly even distribution, wedges of cheese have been swabbed with rubbing alcohol to bring out their color, piping hot sauces are actually ice-cold so that they won't congeal, the grill marks on chicken have been drawn on with Magic Markers, and desserts made of gelatin have been so fortified with artificial thickeners that they are as indestructible as hockey pucks and are often tossed around among the staff, who exhibit the macabre sense of humor of medical students in the morgue, lobbing at each other snowballs of Cool Whip and petrified loaves of shellacked bread. In the case of a famous department store, whose photography department frequently uses baked turkeys as backdrops for their kitchenware, one perfectly preserved carcass was so photogenic that it was used over and over again for eight months until it smelled so badly that the cameramen and art director were forced to wear surgical masks when it was brought out of the refrigerator in all of its gangrenous splendor. As such examples reveal, the beautiful and the delicious are often incompatible, despite consumerism's mistaken, if expedient, attempt to conflate the two. That which appeals to the eye does not necessarily appeal to the tongue, and that which looks revolting, by the same token, is often fit for the consumption of kings. Sculptures belong in museums, not in mouths. It is one of the great ironies of the aesthetic of deliciousness that this exaggeratedly visual style cannot, in the final analysis, be eaten.

THE NATURAL

_____

THE AESTHETIC OF NATURAL FOODS
AND HOLISTIC MEDICINES

H ere is how the chocolate manufacturer Ghirardelli describes its ice cream sundaes:

It starts with a generous scoop of premium almond ice cream, butterscotch topping and golden almond nuggets. Then we add a scoop of premium vanilla ice cream smothered with our home-made hot fudge sauce. . . . So good, it's sinful! . . . It's sure to satisfy your most decadent chocolate cravings. . . . We offer our old creamery ice cream in many tantalizing flavors.

Here is how the magazine *Vegetarian Times* describes one of its desserts:

There's something inherently nurturing about puddings and creams. Soft, soothing and simple, they're
the treats we crave when we want to be especially nice
to ourselves and those we care about. . . . [Puddings
can be eaten] without any guilt whatsoever.

The latter is not a sensual description of food but a social and moral one. Eating is linked, not with the taste
buds, but with the heart, with generosity, with acts of
compassion for oneself and one's friends, who consume a strange therapeutic concoction prepared by a
cook who is more a grandmother than a gastronome.
Only the word "soft" suggests that these magnanimous
puddings actually have texture and flavor, unlike
Ghirardelli's "decadent," "sinful," and "tantalizing" delicacies, which are portrayed as grossly carnal extrava-
gances whose appeal to our baser instincts threatens to
compromise, if only in a teasingly rhetorical way, the
moral well-being of the reprobates who devour them.

Nearly 1,500 years after St. Augustine and the Neo-
Platonists portrayed the body as a contaminated vessel
unsuited for communion with the divine, Western culture still believes that there is an inverse relation between sensuality and saintliness, the pleasures of the

flesh and the destiny of the soul. The look of the natural is rooted in this Judeo-Christian distrust of the senses, this preference for the disincarnate, for "guiltless" puddings that "soothe" and "nurture" rather than "tantalize." Granted, the element of explicit religiosity has disappeared from both eco-marketing in general and the natural foods industry in particular, but the tension between aesthetics and morality lingers on in the conviction that that which tastes good, that which is delicate to the touch and pleasing to the eye, cannot be good for you. After centuries of Gnostic hatred for the body, we continue to fear that such temptations will lead us to perdition or, according to a more modern form of consumerist puritanism, to its contemporary equivalent, the hospital ward where the wages of sin are embolisms, sarcomas, and myocardial infarctions, the dire consequences of greasy sausage links and ice cream fudge bars chock full of saturated fats and bovine growth hormones.

Such patristic zealotry produces its own aesthetic, an anti-aesthetic, a cult of penitential discomfort, of plain brown biodegradable dresses and unbleached "Eco-Tees" made out of stiff, cardboard panels of recycled cotton tinted with environmentally sensitive dyes; lipsticks made of beet juice and face powder of brown oat flour; non-toxic, formaldehyde-free woolen pajamas; and gnarled taproots and misshapen tubers that, while they "have never inspired love at first sight," have "an ugly outer cloak that belies their interior majesty." That which is sensually unappealing has moral authority because the eyes and the tongue have been replaced by the conscience as the primary sensory organ of natural foods, whose healthful, nourishing properties are often directly related to a product's homeliness, to the understated earth-tones of its packaging, to the mousy greys and khaki-beige tans of cold bean curds, vegan root vegetable tempuras, and "soy protein isolate shakes with guaranteed isoflavones."

However venerable the link in Western civilization between iniquity and sensual indulgence, the natural's equation of ugliness and virtuousness has little appeal for a secular society, whose worldview is decidedly agnostic, dependent on the creature comforts of consumerism rather than the incorporeal delights of the celestial realm. As a consequence, manufacturers of natural foods must either perk up their unappetizingly salubrious dishes or risk alienating their markets with products that are all work and no play—tasteless, intellectual exercises in austerity and deprivation that may allay qualms about dwindling rain forests and tortured farm animals but remain fundamentally inedible. Frequently mocked for the politically well-intentioned insipidity of its products, the health foods industry has thus undertaken a concerted campaign to aestheticize nutritious cuisine and dismantle the historic opposition between the body and the soul, as in the case of a devoutly orthodox bistro in New York City (appropriately named The Sanctuary), which serves "nonviolent vegetarian food that also tastes good," the sort of lackluster fare prepared by a chef that one enthusiastic magazine reviewer inadvertently damns with faint praise as "a miracle worker with tofu." The attempt to evoke the wicked pleasures of unholy appetites, while wallowing in the dour rectitude of ugliness, has even created a new type of trompe l'oeil foods: Phoney Baloney, Harmless Ham, the Tempeh Reuben, or the "Unturkey" from Now and Zen, a fake bird made from a sculpted slab of wheat-flour gluten covered in a flesh-like membrane of bean curd. Tofurkey, as it is sometimes called, is the perfect meal for those appalled by atrocities committed against poultry, the universally decried genocide of the chicken coop, which has produced a sort of Save-The-Children fund for domestic fowl: Adopt-a-Turkey, a philanthropic organization that, for a mere $15, enables you to sponsor, like the wide-eyed Central American waifs in magazine ads, your own personal bird languishing on death row, slated for Thanksgiving slaughter. Through the startling paradox of substitute Bratwursts and sloppy joes that offer "everything you liked about meat . . . without the cow!" the natural foods industry would have its bran muffin and eat it too, at once assuaging guilt and offering all the amenities of the Burger Chef, thereby revolutionizing the humorless image of the food Nazi to appeal to a brand-new market of health-foods nuts who refuse to dine solely upon a frugal repast of good intentions.

This attempt to overcome the perceived incompatibility between aesthetics and wholesomeness has run head on into another major problem facing the health foods industry. Concerns have arisen in the minds of many people that consumers are being swindled, despite the claims of those who insist that their secret elixirs of shark cartilage, red sumac, and Dead Sea kelp can reverse hair loss, enlarge breasts, cure impotence, eliminate wrinkles, and reduce cellulite. This crisis of legitimacy has triggered a backlash against the campaign to spice up natural foods and soften the pharisaical image of the conscience-smitten health fanatic. In the very act of making their products more inviting, natural foods manufacturers also attempt to make them more alienating. Featuring sterile rows of hermetically sealed bottles, their advertisements are calculatedly medicinal in appeal, recalling, not so much nature's pantry as the laboratory, the very bastion of conventional medicine, which natural foods manufacturers claim to despise but nonetheless constantly mimic, capitalizing on the reassuringly disinfected look of the hospital. To placate the anxieties of consumers troubled by the disturbing lack of industry regulation, entrepreneurial shamans have removed their feathers and shells and dressed up in white shoes and nurses' smocks, donning stethoscopes and thermometers and speaking to their customers in the confidence-building rhetoric of science, bandying about such terms as "lipids," "bioflavonoids," "hydronical," "chelators," "ionized alkaline microclustered water," "advanced colloidal nutrients," and "actively transported chelate lines."

While the natural foods movement portrays itself as the archenemy of processed foods, in fact it represents the very summit of the industrialization of the kitchen

in the first half of the twentieth century, when manufacturers were as proud of their tin cans as they were of
the cling peaches and Vienna sausages they contained.
The aesthetic of natural foods also elevates the image
of the container, the plastic vitamin jar, the movement's holy grail, which, in advertisements, is constantly depicted floating in mid-air like a spectral
chalice, spilling out the ultimate processed food, the
dietary supplement. Commercials for health products
revolve around the apotheosis of the pill. They often
consist of neat pyramids of pristine white capsules that
are arranged amidst a cornucopia of fruits and vegetables whose rejuvenating properties clever scientists
have managed to distill, concentrating them into easy-
to-swallow lozenges. Again and again, through juxtapositions of vitamins and produce, natural foods
advertisements reenact the consumerist miracle of
compression, of extraction, of miniaturization, of taking all of those brightly colored broccoli florets, pome-
granates, and celery stalks and condensing them into
one unobtrusive tablet, a deceptively small commodity
that houses the entire farm within its fragile sucrose
shell. The image of the universe bursting out of a potentially explosive microcosm is basic to the imagery of

advertising, which endows light-weight, self-contained products, whether it be a Campbell's soup can, a stereo speaker, or the screen of an Apple laptop, with seemingly supernatural powers to harness the forces of nature whose subjugation consumerism celebrates.

Although health foods fanatics are convinced they are going back to the garden and eating wholesome foods that predate DDT, carcinogenic additives, and chemical fertilizers, they are in fact food futurists whose plates are heaped, not with steaming piles of freshly picked squash and string beans, but with copious helpings of space-age pellets. One does not eat these foods, one *takes* them. They do not nourish us, they rev us up, supplying us with the sheer high-caloric bravado we need to face the ordeal of working in the high-pressured corporate environment. The aesthetic of the natural describes the body in mechanistic terms as a complex metal contraption that runs on fuel capsules, on "Immune Rocket Boosters," "Power Drivers," and "high octane" "Superfood," sources of something repeatedly identified as "energy." Vitamin advertisements represent this property with garish sunbursts, zigzagging streaks of lightning, and photographs of laughing, carefree women who leap like gazelles through fields of windswept daffodils. Natural advertisements promote a distinct vision of eating and ingestion, one that conjures up images, not of hard-working farmers sitting down before a gingham-covered table crowded with gravy boats and mounds of mashed potatoes, but of faceless corporate cyborgs plugging themselves into electrical rechargers, reactivating their flagging batteries with a bracing dose of "Brain Pep," a "lab-tested mental energizer," or "power packed" energy shakes like "Rob's Carob Rocket" and "Pam's Papaya Power," miraculous panaceas for a world suffering from the chronic fatigue of ever-more-stressful jobs. As our lives become more hectic and we have less time for the preparation of real foods, consumerism has changed our very concept of eating, which it has conflated with the metaphor of stoking furnaces, of refueling the human gas tank, which burns a combustible propellant that is anything but "natural," having been smelted and refined by the most sophisticated techniques of the fast-foods industry.

The natural not only allies itself with the corporate world and exalts convenience foods but attempts to recreate its traditional market in the image of the conservative go-getter, as can be seen in the publicity photographs of "Taoist internal alchemists" in immaculate three-piece suits, channelers bedizened with ladylike strands of pearls, and colonic therapists wearing bow ties and lapel pins. With their dazzling smiles and perfect coiffures, these bright-eyed-and-bushy-tailed professionals seem ready to jump off the pages of holistic health magazines. The natural foods industry has carefully suppressed the conventional image of the hippie in bell bottoms and tie-dyed T-shirts, wasting away on bark and twigs, and has created instead a prosperous, well-fed image of the rosy-cheeked blonde Baby Boomer who, like any conscientious Fifties mom slaving away in her kitchen, baking TollHouse cookies and tuna-noodle casseroles, treats her ailing children with KidSpritz, "a tasty echinacea spray," and AcidophiKidz, "a chewable tablet that balances your child's digestive system by maintaining friendly flora." In an effort to reach beyond the narrow niche of the hard-core vegetarian fringe, manufacturers use models who avoid even the slightest hint of funkiness, creating a fantasy market of story-book grandmothers dandling fat babies and proud fathers beaming at frisky toddlers splashing in wading pools. Aware of our distrust of aging bohemians, the health foods industry is experimenting with a form of aesthetic recruitment that wins converts by allaying fears that those who eat natural products belong to a distinct sartorial caste of beatniks and flower children who smoke grass and wear Birkenstocks.

A curious vacuum lies at the very heart of the aesthetic of the natural, the conspicuous absence of anything that even remotely resembles nature, which in reality swarms with microbial life, whereas the mythical consumerist nature fabricated by the natural foods movement is as spic-and-span as a laboratory. Our obsession with bottled spring water, "reverse osmosis" faucet filters, air purifiers, and hypoallergenic vacuum sweepers that suck up pollen, pet dander, and dust mites is actually a product of the elevated standards of sterility stimulated by the microscope and our new fear of the unseen, as well as by innovative appliances that have enabled us to achieve unprecedented levels of sanitation in our bathrooms and kitchens. The aesthetics of the holistic health movement enable us to see the unseen. Nowhere is the unnatural nature of the natural more apparent than in countless advertisements for products that perform "colonic irrigation," a type of exorcism by laxative that removes something called "fecal matter build-up," from saber-toothed tape worms to "green globs" of "mucoid plaque" composed of millions of parasite eggs. Both the authors of such books as *Guess What Came to Dinner?* and the manufacturers of such products as Arise & Shine's "Clean-Me-Out-Now" have created a separate aesthetic for representing, in vivid, if anatomically capricious, terms, the infernal regions of the alimentary canal, which are populated by demonic forms. The so-called bowel management industry relies on the imagery of B-grade Hollywood horror flicks to depict the chimeras that feed on our intestines, like those shown in one advertisement that presents "the world's most disgusting picture gallery," a set of nine close-ups of the microscopic Loch Ness monsters that are busily "sucking the life out of us." The ideal of internal cleanliness promoted by colonic irrigants is decidedly unnatural, because human beings have probably hosted these parasites since we first crawled out of the swamp. Such advertisements as the illustration for Chomper's lymphatic drainage system, which shows two outstretched hands perversely proffering a purplish coil of toxic excrement above the Biblical injunction "cleanse thyself," evoke our horror of nature, not our love of it. The entire detoxification movement, with its fruit-juice fasts, herbal enemas, prune purgatives, and water cures, applies the middle-class religion of the impeccable house to the body itself, as if we were, not messy organisms full of blood and guts, but tidy systems of stainless steel valves, plastic tubes, and chrome pipes that must be regularly flushed out through the ingestion of detergents that "act like a broom to 'sweep' from the colon the build-up which accumulated over time," leaving us "clean as a whistle." The natural turns out to be a fiction of bourgeois tidiness created by our pathological involvement with the indoors rather than the outdoors, a desperate campaign to keep nature at bay rather than to embrace it with open arms.

Our alienation from nature is also expressed in the mythology that lies behind vegetarianism: that by consuming leaves, grass, and flowers one is somehow casting off one's mundane self and absorbing the life, beauty, and even the soul of the natural world. Vegetarianism relies on a primitive belief in food animism, an allegorical, Eucharistic notion of eating as a way of gnawing our way out of our cities and restoring our connection with the environment, which has been irreparably damaged by both pollution and the relatively recent termination of any direct involvement with agriculture. By gorging ourselves on dandelion greens and milk-thistle, we achieve intimacy with a deity who, as farmers, we once knew on a daily basis, getting so close to the earth that we actually incorporate parts of it into our body in a symbolic act of cannibalism, much as Catholics dine upon the flesh and blood of their savior to know him more personally, to eliminate the distance that lies between them. As agribusiness assumes complete control over food production and we spend less time out-of-doors, living almost exclusively in the glass bubble of an entirely manmade landscape, eating has become one of the sole ways in which we experience integration with our world, which we no longer encounter out in the fields, laboring with tractors and ploughs under a scorching sun, but at the dinner table, where we labor with forks and spoons, engaging in philosophic acts of righteous mastication. Ingestion thus represents a desperate gesture of intimacy. The bovine religion of the grazing New Age herbivore is a sacramental activity, a breaking of communal bread, a mass performed at the altar of the growling stomach where we stage elaborate rituals that reveal how tenuous our rapport with nature has become. In an effort to escape our confinement, we raven down sunflowers and geraniums, polishing off whole plates of lichens and fern fronds and shoveling into our mouths raw specimens of a world from which we feel cut off, trapped in the desperate biological quarantine in which we have immured ourselves, an anomalous ecosystem that sustains a single life form.

THE AESTHETIC OF NATURE PHOTOGRAPHY
AND THE USES OF LANDSCAPES IN ADVERTISING

John Berger has referred to the modern public zoo, which first appeared in the eighteenth century, as "an epitaph" to our relationship with animals, a signal that they are disappearing from our lives, withdrawing from our farms and houses into cages, leaving us entirely isolated as a species, the last remaining occupants of Noah's Ark. Even pets are no longer animals but homunculi who live in an entirely humanized paradise where they consume the same nutritious foods that we do, eating LifeSource's Holistic Pet Foods, Wow Bow's Vegan doggie treats, and the organic brown rice and freshly milled grains recommended by "veterinarian herbalists." Photographs of exotic beasts and rugged landscapes in both greeting cards and advertisements for everything from cigarettes to Caribbean cruises also provide an epitaph to nature, an Instamatic necropolis that robs the out-of-doors of its inhumanness, much as children's books evoke a world in drag, holding up a flattering mirror that reflects cozy suburban interiors occupied by Mama Bears in aprons and cats in galoshes and sombreros.

While the inter-species transvestism of Hallmark, Magic Moments, and American Greetings is far subtler than that found in Beatrix Potter, *Winnie-the-Pooh,* and *Charlotte's Web,* commercial nature photographers also depict an anthropomorphized world that revolves around propagandistic images of happy nuclear families, of calico kittens nestled against ferocious mastiffs ("Happy Birthday! Hope your day is just purrfect!!") and proboscis monkeys clutching their infants with fiercely possessive maternalism ("I've found love within your arms"). These snapshots of togetherness function simply as allegorical transpositions of our own domestic lives into the jungle and the barnyard. Our favorite nature scenes involve heart-warming pictures of koalas, kangaroos, and polar bears teaching their children the wisdom of the wild, roughhousing during leisure moments, rubbing snouts like Eskimos, or fraternizing peacefully with other denizens of the forest primeval, images free of the grotesque business of scavenging for decomposed carrion, disemboweling prey, or mauling the blind, new-born pups of other species. The ferocity of Darwin's nature has given way to the pabulum of calendar art, since the impermissibly violent rites of rutting and inter-course, to say nothing of the genocidal purging from the pack of the weak, elderly, and deformed, would seem too rapacious for the average viewer, who seeks confir-mation in other primates of the joys of parenthood.

The magnificent nature photography and film con-tained in everything from *Wild Kingdom* to *National Geographic,* from *Smithsonian* to *Jacques Cousteau,* rely on the close-ups taken by the cameraman-voyeur, who per-petrates breathtaking invasions of nature's privacy to get within shooting distance of that nervous flock of marbled gotwits and that chattering herd of Colobus monkeys in Zanzibar. The now commonplace conven-tion of the close-up conceals the fact that, in reality, na-ture is rarely "close-up," that it is secretive, evasive, and unforthcoming, that it flees from us, much as we flee from it, that it jealously protects its own surreptitious-ness and can be glimpsed only from a safe distance with the help of the zoom lens. Modern technology has artificially eliminated the gap between the natural and the human worlds, so that nature's secrets have been betrayed, its lairs transformed into tourist traps through which vicarious sight-seers are led on a kind of guided Beverly Hills tour, trampling through the back-yards of reclusive celebrities, the publicity-shy divas of the endangered species list. The environmental paparazzi have turned the forest and jungle into petting zoos and fostered an artificial chumminess with an environment that remains as inaccessible as ever, separated from us by a wall of inter-species hostility, an insurmountable barrier of fear that only the Polaroid and the Minolta have managed to pierce. Close-ups may have brought us nearer to nature than we have ever been since paleolithic times, but they have also created misunderstandings about the current state of our relation to our environment. They have promoted a peaceable kingdom view of nature, a utopia that exists only on film where, as naturalist couch potatoes, we venture out in our pajamas through our television screens into the Everglades and the Amazon, convinced that those emperor penguins and Galapagos turtles are within *arm's reach*. In fact, however, the aesthetics of the new photographic voyeurism have only made the geographic and psychological distance that separates us invisible, creating an illusory sense of contiguity mediated by such high-tech devices as Bausch & Lomb's binoculars, which "bring the details of life's most adventurous moments into focus," or the Meade ETX Telescope, which allows you to "see every wisp of velvet on the antlers of a deer fifty feet away."

Although the natural makes even the most exotically plumaged cockatiels and brightly colored schools of tropical fish seem as close as our channel-changers, the aesthetic actually indoctrinates us in the opposite belief, that nature is never nearby, never in our backyards, but always somewhere else, somewhere distant, lying forever out of reach in dense equatorial jungles, coral reefs, and Antarctic mountain ranges. Tourism, one of the industries most dependent on the fabrications of the natural, has warped and exoticized our vision of the out-of-doors, which, in an effort to encourage travel, is portrayed in a highly selective way that emphasizes its glamorous remoteness and unapproachability, like an advertisement for Crystal Cruises, whose captain is called "the Prime Minister of Faraway," or a public service announcement that features the menacing face of a noble savage daubed with war paint above a caption that reads "when you think of exotic vegetation, fiery volcanos, and colorful natives, think of Iceland." Commerce has thus had a direct impact on the way that we experience nature, creating paradisial vacation spots that can be reached only by undertaking exorbitantly expensive pilgrimages, five-star luxury crusades stimulated by the proliferation of photographs that bring Australian sea anemones and Bactrian camels from Mongolia right into our living rooms.

Nature photography, like food photography, is in many ways pure pornography. Much as the perfect bodies in stag films interfere with our ability to appreciate our real lovers, photography inflates aesthetic standards applicable to nature and hinders our ability to enjoy our immediate surroundings, which pale in comparison with distant worlds populated by outlandish species of armadillos, aardvarks, and orangutans. The danger of nature pornography is two-fold. Its alluring colors and unearthly forms lead us to neglect the world around us and despise nature in its more commonplace incarnations in the backyard, spoiled as we are by images of humpback whales gamboling amidst icebergs or crustaceans hiding in the Great Barrier Reef. But, perhaps more important, the subliminal message that nature is always far away stimulates curiosity and leads to the invasion of the outback by armies of well-intentioned tourists, who stampede through the wilderness, leaving behind the litter of their picnics and a gory trail of fresh roadkill, riding roughshod over ecosystems threatened by crowds and pollution.

In even the best nature magazines, the subjects selected are those with the most vibrant hues: technicolor flora and fauna in arsenic greens, Titian reds, acid yellows, and shocking pinks, as in an article about "little birds so incredibly blue they seem fragments of some distant magic sky" or in an advertisement for a Pentax Camera that enables you to capture Kenya in "three distinct modes: deep saffron, fiery orange, and crimson." Photographers treat nature as one big paint pot, a chromatic riot that blinds us to the subtlety of the browns and grays of our everyday landscapes, which look positively sallow next to the fly-traps and orchids that have become the botanical centerfolds of *Sierra* and *Natural History*. Such voluptuous pictorial clichés may seem to come straight out of the darkest reaches of the rain forest, but in fact they reflect the unnaturally vivid colors of modern advertisements, which have trained our eyes to expect hues that capture our attention and imprint on our memories the image of the product being sold. The vision of nature presented in magazines is tailored to rival the artists of Madison Avenue, to supply eyes spoiled by the fluorescent tones of consumerism with their chromatic fix, the addictive drug of loud, saturated tints that can be found only in the most exotic reefs and rain forests. Our very conception of what constitutes nature is refracted through the aesthetics of consumerism, which have become the window through which we look at our world. This lush color scheme disciplines the eye, compromises perception, and ultimately leads us to ignore or denigrate more natural colors, which cannot compete with the brilliance of the pixel and the Ben-day dot.

There is another, more literal window through which we observe nature: the windshield, the porthole through which tourists in car advertisements, basking in bucket seats in climate-controlled luxury, watch wild horses galloping by or gaze upon gorges while negotiating hairpin turns on mountain roads. Nature scenes are a staple of PR for the automobile industry, which often presents images of the out-of-doors as seen from the comfort of the indoors, from the standpoint of the rich leather upholstery and deep-pile wool carpets of a vehicle that is nothing less than a drawing room on wheels. The aesthetic of car advertisements is often based on dramatic contrasts between the alligators and grizzly bears that lie beyond the windows, snapping at the radial tires and pawing at the hood, and serene interiors in which motorists relax to the classical music from their surround-sound stereo systems, like those found in the Lincoln Navigator, "the first full-size sport utility to take luxury deep into the great outdoors."

The more destructive a product is to either the environment or our own bodies, the more prominently images of nature figure in the way it is advertised, as can be seen in ubiquitous billboards and subway posters for cigarettes, alcohol, and cars, all of which feature picturesque waterfalls and mist-enshrouded groves of giant sequoias. Advertisers use nature much as they use children, as the detergent for morally problematic commodities, a way of sanitizing lead emissions, smog, emphysema, and sclerosis of the liver. As a result of this attempt to offset a product's unsavory reputation with a purifying dose of counter-iconography, the aesthetic of the natural is rife with non sequiturs, with pictorial discontinuities: bottles of Absolut Vodka stranded inappropriately in the middle of a rocky desert; jeeps perched precariously atop inaccessible cliffs in the Himalayas; range ovens busily cooking away in the bayous beneath spreading oak trees draped with Spanish moss; and Timex watches wrapped, not around wrists, but around branches in a forest. With such jarringly irrelevant imagery and text (the Timex ad reads "Green grass. Rolling hills. Fresh air. Open seven days a week"), advertisements often struggle to suppress the distinction between the manmade and the artificial, to "naturalize" the machine, to make believe that that "home theater system" and that washer and dryer plopped down in the middle of a meadow are actually found objects spotted by chance roaming about in the wild. Manufacturers use leaves and twigs as a literal form of camouflage, the olive drab in which Madison Avenue dresses up products so that they seem perfectly compatible with nature, if not indistinguishable from it. Advertisements now conflate basic categories of the mechanical and the organic through visual conceits that simply juxtapose the plastic of computer terminals or the galvanized steel of cars with the petals of flowers or the trunks of trees. In the face of objections that industry is destroying the environment, consumerism has learned to erase itself, to take on the protective coloration of its ideological surroundings, to fend off its Leftist predators and blend into the ever more strident chorus of complaints being registered against it.

One of the most striking non sequiturs in advertisements is the automobile, which appears as frequently off-road as it does on, parked in forest clearings and boggy fens or racing, not over concrete and asphalt, but over mudflats and fields of sunflowers. The aesthetic of car advertisements relies on a central metaphor, that of the restive driver who has left the beaten path, strayed from interstate turnpikes choked with traffic, and entered a realm of rugged individuality, "the other side of the hill," which can be reached only by the owners of Pontiac Montanas who are "interested in taking a spirited, more adventurous path through life." One wistfully facetious advertisement features a mountain man with a scraggly, Rip Van Wrinkle beard, the proud owner of a Honda CRV and the author of a book entitled *Free the Caveman Within You,* the "authoritative guide to unlocking your primitive instincts" ("learn how to turn your modern world into a place where your wild side can roam free"). Car advertisements are allegories in which pavement represents the decadent world of civilization, where obedient motorists speed down life's superhighway or sit mired in the gridlock of their thwarted ambitions. Forest settings or overgrown dirt trails that churn up clouds of dust, on the other hand, represent the untamed wilderness where one undertakes the typical consumerist journey, a voyage of self-discovery that involves strategic purchases that strengthen one's individuality. Ironically, the one modern invention that, perhaps more than any other, has severed our connection with nature and polluted the environment, poisoning the air and tearing rents in the ozone layer, is portrayed as one of the only available means of getting back in touch with nature and forging a unique personality in the face of mass conformity.

The animistic cults of primitive man were based on his dependence on nature, which he reified as a capricious spirit, a malevolent power that was so vindictive that it thought nothing of obliterating careless votaries for even minor infractions of sacrificial etiquette or dietary laws, wreaking havoc by unleashing droughts, famines, and floods. This religious attitude toward nature sprang from our fear of its irrationality, its foul temper, a volatility that inspired the first narratives of Western culture, elaborate myths about jealous deities hurling thunderbolts. After the Renaissance, the religious and animistic attitude toward nature gave way to the opposite point of view, the aesthetic attitude, in which nature is portrayed as an innocuous spectacle designed for our entertainment, an immense diorama so beautiful that one public service announcement calls it "a masterpiece displayed on a fragile museum called Earth." The aesthetic attitude toward nature becomes possible only when we have vanquished the environment, when it does our bidding, when we feel immune to its caprices, and hence have the leisure to admire the subtlety of its hues and the infinite variety of its forms, as in countless advertisements that feature images of contemplative hikers standing passively on cliffs overlooking huge expanses of rocky terrain while wearing cutting-edge walking shoes and carrying cell phones with global satellite link-ups. Ironically, as we have seen in the representation of cyberspace, if animistic religions play any role in contemporary culture at all, they now explain the bewildering incoherence and arbitrariness of something that is the exact opposite of nature—machines, which have become the new irrational deities of our daily lives, tormenting us, not with earthquakes and tornadoes, but with corporate cataclysms: short-circuited modems, virus-infected diskettes, power surges, and crashed hard drives. We have come full circle and the terror we once experienced at the prospect of disasters like bubonic plagues and climate changes is now directed toward our own tools, especially towards the computer, the sinister muse of the latest animistic religion.

Nature has now been so thoroughly sapped of its power to intimidate us that we view its clear blue skies and crystalline lakes as nothing more than placid sanctuaries for psychological refreshment, where we wind down with tapes that lull us to sleep with recordings of babbling brooks and the wind soughing through the trees, "sounds [that] help wash away tension and set the mood for a pleasant, pressure-free mental break." The natural is the product of a society in desperate need of relaxation, so anxious and high-strung that it uses the out-of-doors as if it were simply a rest cure for candidates for cardiac arrest, vexed businessmen who are assured that "people who vacation in California enjoy 39% more inner peace." When seen in light of the promises made by the manufacturers of natural foods that their products will "jump-start your morning," "supercharge your entire body," and "restore your stamina so you can go, go, go all day," giving you the "physical endurance to climb mountains, sky dive, or run a marathon!", the aesthetic of the natural is strangely contradictory. It simultaneously revs us up and slows us down, feeds us energy pills that allow us to tackle our daily chores at the office at breakneck speeds and then plunges us into Saltwater Flotation Spas where we can recuperate from the madness, lying in a drugged, semi-comatose state of collapse, using Celestial Seasonings new Herbal Supplements to "nurture your body and soothe your soul" or Aura Cacia Aromatherapy that lets you "bathe in the beauty of nature." Images in advertisements of people soaking in bath tubs full of organic sea salts, lying in canoes, their fingers dabbling in the waters of peaceful holiday resorts, and smoking the "best cigarette of the day," their feet propped up on the porch of a log cabin, are full of the distress and unease caused by tensions in the workplace. A Baconian scream rips through the peace of Madison Avenue's quiet clearings. Long ago, mankind took shelter from nature in his own manmade world. Now he takes shelter from the manmade world in nature, or at least in a simulacrum of nature, a New Age health spa that we have created in the opposite image of the high-pressured corporate world.

GLAMOROUSNESS

T he toxin produced by the botulinum bacillus can increasingly be found, not only in the biological weapons arsenal of Saddam Hussein, but in the medicine cabinets of respectable dermatologists and high-society plastic surgeons. While in the hands of careless cooks and international terrorists botulism causes paralysis, convulsive vomiting, respiratory failure, and even sudden death, the bacterium works like a vanishing cream when injected in minute doses directly into deeply creased frown lines and crow's-feet, which relax as tiny facial muscles are anesthetized for months at a time, unable to contract when those who submit to the treatment smile, laugh, cry, scowl, or even scream. This hieratic look requires regular booster shots which, on a number of unfortunate occasions, have seeped through the capillaries into the eyelids, creating the heavily medicated appearance of a sad-eyed cocker spaniel.

While few women are willing to submit to the discomfort, inconvenience, and expense of the "Botox facelift" (crow's-feet are zapped for $500, furrowed brows for $750, leathery, Kate Hepburn necks for $1,000), many consumers are quite eager to ingest another sort of toxin, the photographs in women's magazines, which also specialize in impassive, expressionless faces. When women freeze their features with botulism injections, they are not only attempting to reverse the ravages of time but also to recreate in flesh and blood conventions derived from advertising and photography, incorporating into their expressions and gestures the iconography of the commercial.

Throughout the history of women's magazines, the idealized face of the model has always concealed an unspoken ultimatum. Glowering accusingly at the reader, this alabaster mask intimidates her into buying products that cosmetic companies offer as a form of facial blackmail, the talismans she is led to believe will overcome her own insecurity, as well as the model's inexplicable unfriendliness. Beneath the latter's icy hauteur and flawless complexion is another sort of face altogether, the implied face, the hypothetical face of the reader, a despicable crone who, in the early twentieth century, was relegated to the back pages of magazines like *Vogue*. The ravaged features of this pariah are afflicted with a nightmarish array of dermatological disorders, the lurid subjects of vintage advertisements for things like the "Ganesh Chin Strap," a muzzle that cured double chins by holding the jaw shut while sleeping to prevent the "unsanitary" habit of snoring; the "Hydro Vacu," which sucked out blackheads and "skin eruptions" with a tiny suction cup; "Mme. Julian's Specific," which removed the "superfluous hair" shown in a drawing of a bearded lady with a full mustache and goatee; or "Cuticura Soap," a "treatment for torturing, disfiguring, itching, burning, bleeding, scaly, crusted, and pimply skin and skalp humours, eczemas, rashes, irritations, small pox scars . . . and moth patches." Even the manufacturers of Wrigley's Double Mint Gum attempted to capitalize on the undercurrent of anxiety so crucial to glamor by suggesting that gum-chewing strengthened facial muscles and thus "ward[ed] off flabby wrinkles about the mouth." The more monolithic and porcelain-like the sardonic faces of the models became, the more decrepit grew the mythical consumer's face, the anti-face represented in turn-of-the-century advertisements, which provide a cautionary portrait of a woman who had failed to heed the cosmetic industry's apocalyptic warnings.

Intimidation also comes in less obvious forms. One of the most important "scenes" in the narrative of the contemporary fashion advertisement involves a woman who is usually photographed mid-stride casting back over her shoulder a look of contempt or indifference at someone who seems to be calling out to her from an implied male viewpoint. If it is possible to say that something as static as a photograph has a story line, the "action" or "plot" of the typical advertisement in *Vogue* takes place in the model's peripheral vision. Here, we are often encouraged to imagine an invisible suitor who is importuning her, summoning her, pestering her with unsolicited invitations, which she acknowledges, not by pivoting her entire body and facing the intruder directly, but by looking at him askance with only a perfunctory and dismissive turn of the head, all the while pretending, as she runs a gauntlet of excited men (made all the more real by their absence), that she is aloof, preoccupied, alone. In an advertisement for

Nordstrom Department Store, a model wearing a pristine white dress, referred to as "a gathering of gossamer blooms," is shown walking briskly down a sidewalk as she angrily jerks the hem of her skirt, which billows out in a graceful ripple, as if she had just snatched it out of someone's grip. Twisting her head nearly 180 degrees, this sullen beauty confronts her implicit assailant with a look so ferocious that the viewer can almost see the men who are shadowing her just beyond the margins of the photograph, stalking her with a thankless devotion intensified by her air of scornful self-sufficiency. When we flip through the pages of *Vogue*, we are often watching the fashion model being watched herself in a scenario that stages one of the reader's central fantasies, that of the begrudging acceptance of someone's homage, a fantasy made all the more seductive by the fact that the model seems to be indifferent to—or even irritated by—the very thing the reader consults the fashion magazine to learn: how to be desirable. In the interrupted woman's disdain for her infatuated pursuer, the reader is treated to the ultimate form of glamor, the glamor of rejection, of models so confident of their own mystique that they seem to despise what the reader herself values highly, the attention of men.

The effect of glamor on the consumer has been intensified by changes that have occurred in the media in the last few decades. Only during the 1950s did photographs entirely supplant illustrations as the primary means of advertising clothing, a revolution that, if slow in the making, radically altered the psychological relationship of the model to the reader. Until this time, glamor inhered less in the face of the drawing, which was by necessity schematic and generalized, than in the sketch's attitude, posture, and gestures, especially in the strangely dainty positions of the hands. Glamor once resided so emphatically in the stance of the model that the faces of the illustrations cannot really be said to have expressions at all, but angles or tilts: the chin raised upwards in a haughty look; the eyes lowered in an attitude of pious introspection; the head cocked at an inquisitive or coquettish angle; or the profile presented in sharp outline, emanating power and severity like an emperor's bust embossed on a Roman coin. "Expression" was thus once achieved not by changing the features but by pivoting the entire head. Up until the time photography finally prevailed in women's magazines, the whole history of the representation of the face was antithetical to expression, so that glamor tends to be by tradition "faceless," both because the features of the drawing were hard to individualize and because expression detracted from the totemic presence of the model as an august "type." Long after advertisers realized the economic advantages of creating the allure of a unique presence, conventions of rigidity and blankness that arose from the association of fashion with graphically imprecise drawings linger on as a remnant of this older tradition, tending to foster a look of vacancy in a photographic medium versatile enough to capture a wide range of expressions. Fashion designers now even incorporate into their seasonal product line launches modernist images of ur-marionettes, as in the case of Dutch wunderkind Walter Van Beirendonck, who sews cloth masks over his models' faces and dresses them as androids who lumber down the runway on aluminum stilts until they fall off the end of the catwalk like lemmings or broken windup toys, landing in a disordered pile at the paparazzi's feet.

Starting in the 1930s and 1940s and finally prevailing in the 1950s, the techniques of what might be called the "Age of the Face" gained wider and wider currency as the dominant method of marketing clothing. This new trend in fashion photography shifted the location of the model's power from her body and gestures to her face and expressions, a displacement of focus that by necessity thrust on the reader the model's identity, her specific as opposed to generic nature. Throughout the 1940s and 1950s, the face grew incrementally in size until, by the 1960s, it frequently filled an entire page—as it does today in such advertisements as the two full pages devoted to Bijan perfume, one showing a swarthy, enigmatic woman enshrouded in an Islamic chador, who looks at once submissive and unfathomable, and the other showing a boisterous American tomboy wearing a baseball cap and holding a bat as she screams at the top of her lungs in a way that suggests that, in contrast to her inscrutable Middle Eastern counterpart, she is "bright, wild, flirty, fun, eccentric, tough, bold, and very, very Bijan." Unlike the aesthetic of exclusion, which deliberately fosters a relation of inequality between the viewer and the model, the aesthetic developed in the Age of the Face emphasizes communication and directness. Existing side by side with a diametrically opposite marketing technique (which it doesn't so much contradict as complement), the aesthetic of inclusion minimizes the distance between the reader and the ad and even attempts to achieve a riveting impression of physical confrontation through a kind of trompe l'oeil effect created by the size of the face and the hypnotic fixity of the gaze. In L'Oreal's advertisement for "Hydra Perfecte," for example, the actress and model Andie MacDowell looks out at us compassionately as she rests her chin on her fists, a pose so suggestive of candor and empathy that she appears to be inviting us to talk to her about our problems. While scornfulness still remains an essential way of advertising products, a new, antithetical method has grown up beside it that now repositions the reader and the model in such a way that they *literally* "face" each other, as women and as peers.

The aesthetic of inclusion is not a recent invention. As early as the 1930s, open smiles suggesting an indigenous style of American beauty, the corn-fed Kansas look of an artless good girl ("sexy sans sin," as one advertising executive put it), began appearing right next to the bitchy ice maidens whose glacial tranquillity is what we naturally think of as the characteristic expression of the fashion model. As the face became more important to marketing, many advertising agents, like those at Grey Advertising, who designed the Cover Girl campaign,

sought "to approach but not cross that fine line between the beauty women will relate to and crave and the
beauty women will be jealous of, find contemptuous, or
ignore." A statement like the following, by Mike Litman,
an executive at Grey, epitomizes recent efforts to promote friendliness and thus counteract, or at least sub-
due, the disconcerting effect of glamor, its potential to
backfire and repel the viewer, inspiring disobedience or
intractability rather than intimidating her into a state of
passive readiness to consume:

> I like to think about, you know, how one of these mod-
> els would get along with my wife. I mean whether they
> would actually talk if they met at a party, and if my wife
> would say, "Wow, she was really nice." Now with Carol
> [a famous model]—well, it turns out my wife really
> likes Carol. I've introduced them, and she thinks she's
> really nice.

On the March 1992 cover of *Vogue*, the rhetoric of
"niceness" finds one of its most effective expressions in
a photograph (deliberately reminiscent of Botticelli's
Venus) of a magnificent blonde with a robust, rosy-
cheeked style of American beauty whose face radiates a

sincerity guaranteed to withstand the skepticism and jealous rancor of even the most vigilant wives.

The beguilingly sweet and sisterly smiles that start appearing on the faces of models as photography gains the upper hand over illustrations do not, however, represent a genuine improvement in the coercive nature of facial politics but rather deprive readers of one of their natural defenses against glamor. To maintain our sense of the value and integrity of our own lives, we have allowed ourselves, as members of a society propelled by the forces of envy, to denigrate beauty as a state of stupidity, loneliness, unhappiness, shallowness, and self-preoccupation, a hypothetical state of misery that embodies our resentful, Judeo-Christian suspicions of the body. Increasingly, the advertiser is attacking the very foundation of Western moralizations about attractiveness, thus undermining the psychological immunity we have developed to control its power over us and to protect ourselves from the feelings of self-loathing it inspires. Far from looking isolated and unhappy, the contemporary model often looks nice, polite, and gregarious—a woman we are encouraged to think of as an ally, a confidante, a pal, an individual of such irreproachable integrity that she immediately thwarts our efforts to dismiss her as a vapid femme fatale as empty as she is ravishing. And yet in the final analysis, the bullying effect on the viewer of her cloying likableness is much the same as the effect of contempt: Both produce helplessness before glamor, one by demoralizing us, the other by depriving us of consoling stereotypes about beauty as old as Western culture itself, stereotypes that have served a vital function of suppressing resentment.

Advertisers have not been content simply to offset the traditional remoteness of the fashion model by providing an abundance of compensatory smiles. As the sexual revolution of the 1960s began to increase our tolerance of the public expression of sexuality, a new quasi-pornographic aesthetic started appearing in fashion magazines, where advertisers took the insipidity of the happy face one step further to create the orgasmic face, whose expression is indistinguishable from the highest state of sexual arousal. Such photographs are often in soft-focus, purveying a moist, dewy sensuality, and represent the face tilted upwards, the eyes half-closed, the lips parted to reveal the teeth (if never the tongue, the final taboo of the fashion magazine, an organ that remains discreetly out of sight even when the model seems to heave and shudder through a convulsive climax). In a 1960s advertisement for Abano Perfumed Bath Oil, a woman with her arms wrapped voluptuously over her bare chest revels in her sensuality in front of us, "drift[ing] in a scented dream world." Similarly, a model dressed only in $1,650 hot pants and a $550 pair of "glacé sandal[s] with diamanté buckles" seems so excited to be wearing the creations of a famous footwear designer (whose personality is "as effervescent and surprising as his shoes") that she lies on the floor, swooning in an erotic trance, her left knee lifted to her waist as if she were experiencing uncontrollable passion. With the recent emphasis on the orgasmic face, glamor has acquired an invasive new dimension: The model not only looks splendid, she feels splendid as well, living far more intensely than we do and enjoying a quality of life far superior to our own. As she engages in a sexual demonstrativeness meant to exclude us from the solipsistic intensity of her pleasure, we are confronted with a new form of coercion in the promise her face seems to hold out to us: that glamor brings not only power and seductiveness but also a kind of delirium.

To understand the nature of this new, ostensibly more democratic aesthetic that focuses the reader's attention squarely on the face, it is important to remember that since its inception the whole purpose of the fashion industry has been to compel the reader to imitate the model. The basic assumption of women's magazines is that we can acquire the power of glamor, its omnipotence and invulnerability, by donning the sacred articles of the mannequin's clothing and mimicking her hieratic gestures—a fetishism we associate with primitive religions rather than with a sophisticated secular culture like our own. A fundamental change has occurred, however, that complicates this simple act of fetishism. As attention shifted away from the body and companies began to scour the globe in search of the perfect *face*, squandering millions to locate exactly the right woman to represent their product, the model's chief attraction became her individuality, something that cannot be duplicated. Every year, Cover Girl invests in the neighborhood of $60,000,000 on talent scouting, a laborious, international treasure hunt that one industry analyst estimates costs as much as $119 per facial pore of each of the seven models finally chosen to advertise only four of the company's products: Clean Make-Up, NailSlicks, Continuous Color, and Lip Softeners. Before the 1960s, faces were more or less interchangeable and models were used much as Hitchcock used his actors: as props, nameless professionals available in large numbers at relatively low cost. When Cover Girl launched its unprecedentedly expensive campaign in 1961, however, the model's face quickly became such a priceless commodity that a celebrity system developed around the first fashion superstars, women like Cybill Shepherd, Cheryl Tiegs, and Christie Brinkley, the precursors of Cindy Crawford, Claudia Schiffer, and Christy Turlington, who now receive as much as $10,000,000 a year for their modeling.

The fact that the cosmetic and clothing industries are now using faces of exceptional beauty and, by implication, of extraordinary rarity, would seem to call into question the whole mimetic function of fashion, in that advertisers create the allure of a product by conjuring up the aura of an uncommon and inestimably precious asset, an irreplaceable object that cannot be reproduced. In other words, in the Age of the Face, the new model seems to preclude from the beginning the very act of imitation she invites, an act that common sense tells us would be more easily performed using as a paradigm the facelessness of the anonymous fashion idol, the Hitchockian prop whose interchangeability lends itself more readily to being impersonated.

The advantages of this paradox, of using the unre-producibility of the new $119-per-pore face to promote imitation, is that it obscures the slavish acts of self-effacement and conformity we must perform to acquire glamor. The uniqueness of the contemporary fashion model, a woman who is now as original and distinctive as the turn-of-the-century model was generic and representative, plays a vital role in sustaining *the* central myth of consumerism: that by participating in this most social of activities and by dutifully rigging oneself out in the seasonal uniforms of the tribe, one will acquire, through an almost shamanistic process of transference, the irreducible singularity, the allure, the cachet of the model, the one-of-a-kind art object whose value inheres in its scarcity. The new emphasis on the individuality of the photographic face thus disguises the psychological self-deception involved in glamor; in the act of conforming to prevailing fashions, the reader feels that she is becoming, not less individual and more acquiescent—a docile and fastidious observer of the complex etiquette and arcane proprieties of glamor—but wholly unusual, a rebel, a pioneer, a maverick, a woman as full of uncompromising selfhood as the million-dollar face on the page. Coercion to conform is thus recharacterized as license to express, with the result that the imitative and fundamentally demeaning relation between the model and the reader, a compulsory and manipulative bond intolerant of individual initiative, is discreetly obfuscated.

If the faces of fashion models are often wooden and totemic, their bodies are often strangely elastic, their shoulders hunched, their legs spread in unladylike poses, their rear ends stuck provocatively in the air, their feet, clad in strappy Manolo Blahnik stiletto sandals, thrust out at the reader like those of kickboxers. The unflinching fixity of many models' faces stands in marked contrast to their agitated bodies, which are perpetually off balance, always on the verge of taking an unglamorous pratfall, their arms grasping helplessly in the air for support, their hips cocked so far to one side that it seems impossible that they can maintain their equilibrium for more than a few seconds before they crash to the floor in all of their costly splendor, their Sally Penn black cobra tube dress a bedraggled ruin.

Unlike the prim little ladies in early twentieth-century fashion magazines, who stood bolt upright, the obedient valedictorians of posture-training classes at finishing school, the contemporary model is a slouch

225

who slumps in chairs, brazenly straddles fire hydrants, and sprawls on street curbs, oblivious to the damage being done to her white silk shantung "cocoon" dress and her canary yellow tuxedo pants. What's more, she is frequently careless about her grooming, specifically, about her hair, which can be as tangled as a rag doll's, a windswept rat's nest of frazzled split ends, as if she had just participated in a high-speed chase in a convertible. Bad posture and bad grooming are key components of contemporary glamor because they exhibit the contempt that this sylph-like slob feels for the dress she is wearing, a blasé attitude that sends an unequivocal message to readers that that woman in the snakeskin Versace dress and Medusa curls is *above* posing, *above* trying to look good, *above* conforming to social expectations. Her languid stances and disheveled appearance serve an explicitly ideological function, that of showing how little glamor matters to her, how she holds in disdain the very thing her admirers most desire: to make certain that they look perfect, that when they venture out of doors every hair is in place, that their pantyhose don't sag, that the straps of their bras don't show, that their slips aren't hanging raggedly below their hemlines, and even, in the case of the most

fanatical of fashion fetishists, that the color of their fin-
gernail polish is coordinated with their lipstick, their
belt buckles with their earrings. The contemporary
fashion plate is a make-believe enemy of the very aesthetic she embodies, a law unto herself, a rebel who is
constantly flouting traditionally feminine poses and impossibly ornate coiffures, disobeying the strictures that
the consumer must follow to the letter even as she en-
vies the model's license to transgress the intricate and
constantly changing regulations that make dressing
such a risky enterprise.

While manufacturers have devised subtle ways of lur-
ing the consumer, only the most affluent people can
actually afford to buy the clothing and accessories advertised in *Vogue*. The outfits of models pouting in
chain-mail mini-skirts or strutting bare-chested down
the catwalk in conservative business suits unbuttoned
to the waist bear little resemblance to the wrinkled
khakis, Lacoste shirts, down parkas, and baggy Polo
sweaters found in most women's closets. In fact, just as
the "wondrously articulated classic sauces" and the
"coconut-milk broth [that] smooths the dissonant
notes of fiery chiles" in *Bon Appetit* and *Gourmet* bear an
inverse relation to what we really eat—the "big ol' juicy

frozen pizzas" and the "bakeless wonders" of Freezer Queen TV dinners—so the gold metallic catsuits and embroidered Bill Blass mousseline dresses in *Vogue* and *W* bear an inverse relation to our Levis and loafers. Moreover, just as food magazines provide a form of vicarious eating for a dietetic age, one that no longer has the time to cook for itself, so fashion magazines provide a form of vicarious dressing for a world that no longer has the time to dress itself but prefers the comfortable informality of Tommy Hilfiger's tracksuits and DKNY's tank tops to the unaffordable aggravation of haute couture. Such publications as *Elle* and *Allure* offer a form of sartorial pornography for an era that rejects the inconvenience of elaborate dressing and embraces the inexpensive casualwear mass produced in Taiwanese sweatshops, but nonetheless still longs for a world in which everything is handmade, much as food magazines invent a culinary utopia in which everything is prepared from scratch. The more bland and uniform our clothing becomes, the more outrageously individual are the costumes in fashion magazines. If the exaggeratedly visual aesthetic of deliciousness cannot be eaten, the cumbersomely "artistic" aesthetic of glamor cannot be worn.

Glamor's highly aesthetic attitude toward the woman's body is in part a reaction to the highly sexual attitude that has prevailed throughout the centuries. The audience of glamor is not, as one might expect, men, who are oblivious to its indiscernible subtleties, to minute differences between eye shadows and hair dyes (which can be adjusted by calling L'Oreal's and Clairol's 800 hotlines, whose specially trained operators are standing by to pacify panic-stricken customers in the throes of "coloring crises," horrified to discover that the "light golden red" of Desert Sunrise turned their hair a fiery orange and the "medium burgundy" of Rhubarb an iridescent purple). Instead, the real audience of glamor is other women, who engage in a form of visual lesbianism, submitting themselves to the peer review of fellow connoisseurs who judge each other according to a higher aesthetic standard than mere sex appeal. Arousal is not the primary purpose of glamor. The more appropriate response is admiration, the dispassionate assessment of an audience that, scrupulously adhering to the uncompromisingly aesthetic doctrine of fashion-for-fashion's-sake, enjoys the nuances of glamor, not as aphrodisiacs, the tools of the temptress's trade, but as ends in themselves. Food advertisers avoid mentioning hunger in their commercials to enhance the prestige of their creamed corns and beef stews, which must be "selected" from towering pyramids of cans for the sake of their deliciousness and not for their ability to satisfy the indiscriminate demands of a growling stomach. Similarly, glamor eschews the whole issue of sex appeal, de-emphasizing its utility as a technique for satisfying the indiscriminate demands of lust and turning women into kinetic sculptures, with one form of objectification replacing another, a relentlessly sexual vision of their bodies giving way to a relentlessly aesthetic one. Indeed, for those truly obsessed with fashion, the ultimate audience of glamor is the homosexual—the gay designer, photographer, and makeup artist—who is entirely immune to feminine sensuality and hence judges the latest "It" girl's stylishness as if our Cheryl Tiegses and Christie Turlingtons were mere pieces of furniture upholstered in flesh.

Just as deliciousness is actually nauseating and cuteness is grotesque, so glamor is also indistinguishable from *its* opposite: the gauche and unpoised. It is constantly morphing into the ridiculous, the gratuitously novel, not only because Andrew Grove's burning hairdos, which smolder for hours like outdoor barbecue grills, or see-through nylon trousers with one leg longer than the other reflect the madly permissive clothing of rock stars and Hollywood personalities desperate to grab every column inch they can, but because it is easier to render out-of-date that which is capricious and extravagant than that which is staid and sedate. Conservative clothing remains in style far longer than daring designer "creations." Glamor is a Janus-faced aesthetic that deliberately narrows the boundary between the elegant and the grotesque, frequently obliterating it altogether, making the chic patently absurd.

The madcap spirit of haute couture is crucial to the psychology of dating and its economic corollary, *up*dating, which regularly requires the consumer to weed out the anachronisms of her closet, the hand-me-downs that, during periodic purges, are donated in mint condition to the Goodwill and the Salvation Army. Glamor promises complete license, complete freedom—anything goes, be yourself, do your own thing, get in touch with your outrageousness—and then, without warning, withdraws this permission, leaving the consumer to fend for herself in that Christian Dior tulle-veiled boater bonnet whose brim is as broad as a satellite dish or that topiary hairdo that sits atop her head like an obelisk. The ridiculousness of the aesthetic of glamor

231

aids in this de-conversion process, which turns women into malcontents always scheming against their own wardrobes and thus keeps them returning to department stores to repair the damage inflicted on their sense of personal style by this vicious cycle of permissiveness followed by prescriptiveness, of license followed by humiliation. After getting them into their garments, manufacturers just as quickly get them out of them, suddenly pulling the wool off their eyes and, like Cinderella after midnight, transforming their previously splendid raiment into threadbare rags.

CLEANNESS

D irtiness has physical characteristics but cleanness does not. When something is dirty we see dusty smudges, we feel the grimy patina of grease mixed with soot, and we smell the odors wafting up from garbage cans overflowing with scraps of meat or from vegetables liquefying in our crisper drawers. Cleanness, however, is simply an absence of qualities, an absence of stains, tacky to the touch, an absence of the pungent aromas that assault us when we open a quart of curdled milk, unfold a mildewed rag, or pry too deeply into the debris moldering in the dank regions beneath our kitchen sinks.

Manufacturers of cleaning products, however, would have us believe otherwise, that washing something brings out its sensual properties rather than simply eliminates them, that Mr. Clean makes your toilet bowl smell like "a field of wildflowers blowing in the wind," that Tide imbues your clothes with the "scent of crisp mountain air," and that Colgate "leaves your teeth sparkling white," while Gain creates "whites that wow." In this sense, the rhetoric of cleanness is strikingly similar to the rhetoric of deliciousness. In the case of the aesthetic of food, advertisers circumvent the difficulties of representing such an elusive experience as taste by talking dirty to the consumer and exaggerating the act of chewing, swallowing, and ingesting, providing television audiences, salivating on their sofas, with a vicarious tongue. In the case of representing something as imperceptible as cleanness, manufacturers don't engage in dirty talk, but, more appropriately, in its sanitized equivalent, in clean talk, a way of endowing an invisible state with a marketable set of properties, whether it be the lurid color of a bathroom bowl deodorizer that "blues with each flush, so you know it's cleaning" or the cloying perfumes in soaps that "smell good enough to eat" and toilet paper dispensers rigged with a potent fumigating device that gives off "an extra burst of freshness with every spin."

The problems involved in selling something that cannot be detected with the senses have profound aesthetic consequences for advertising. Faced with the
unglamorous task of persuading people to buy products whose function is purely negative, namely, to get
rid of dirt, companies have devised an imaginary, exhibitionistic type of cleanliness that we can see and smell,
a glittering mirage that makes an emphatic impression
on our bodies and seduces us with its lustrous sheen
and mirror-like polish, thus reassuring us that we have
indeed gotten something for our money.

Cleanness has, for instance, transformed the nose
into the primary sensory organ for detecting sterility,
the exquisitely sensitive instrument with which vigilant
housekeepers sniff anxiously about their kitchens like
bloodhounds. In an effort to make a freshly laundered
blouse or a well-mopped kitchen appeal to our imaginations as vividly as a fetid pile of rags or a scuffed
linoleum floor, advertisers promote the fiction that the
essentially odorless state of cleanness has a distinct
smell, that tidiness is as aromatic as dirtiness is mal-
odorous, a fiction they construct by doctoring their detergents with over-powering fragrances that are
"country fresh," "rain fresh," "pine fresh," "baby-

powder fresh," "rose-petal fresh," and "fresh, like a cool mountain stream." Moreover, according to the false sensuality of the immaculate, we can not only smell cleanness but hear it (hair is described as "squeaky clean," sheets as "crisp and crackling") and, what's more, feel it (as in the case of such an irresistibly squeezable product as Charmin Toilet Paper or Ultra Snuggle Laundry Detergent, whose mascot is a fuzzy teddy bear that promises to make our clothing as downy soft as a plush animal). The fruit names of air fresheners ("Tropical Nectar," "Citrus Sunrise," "Green Apple") also suggest that cleanness appeals to the consumer's taste buds—a grotesque idea because even the most fastidious housewives refrain from licking their bathtubs and commodes after they have swabbed them out with lemon-scented Lysol or cherry Blossom Bowl cleaner. Consumerism has dramatically expanded the way we react to cleanness, making something as inconspicuous and unappealing as the antiseptic an all-encompassing sensual experience that triggers a barrage of vivid stimuli. By filling their bottles with potentially toxic additives that elicit tactile responses, manufacturers have complicated and therefore heightened our awareness of cleanness, which we no longer define as the mere absence of grime but as the *presence* of heady perfumes, garish dyes, and fabric softeners, the superfluous new prerequisites of hygiene. Such cosmetic features have lowered our tolerance for dirt and raised our standards of sanitation, spoiling our senses and enslaving us to products that have created entirely new ways of perceiving dust mops, wet sponges, and pails of soapy water, the banal munitions of housework.

Among the prominent aesthetic features of cleanness are suds, a thick lather of foam that, while playing an insignificant role in the actual process of laundering clothes or washing dishes, plays a major psychological role in reminding the consumer that, beneath a detergent's frothy effervescence, a purifying chemical reaction is indeed occurring. In the first half of the century, billowing clouds of pink bubbles were essential to products like Super Suds, which gave "you suds in a flash" or Chipso Quick Suds, which produced, "not thin listless suds, [but] *lasting* suds," unlike their competitors' detergents which, rather than boiling over in torrents of sweet-smelling fizz, sank to the bottom of stagnant sinks full of cloudy water covered in an iridescent slick of oil. As ecology has made us more conscious of the destructive effects of phosphates on the environment, however, the whole aesthetic of cleanness has been revolutionized and soap bubbles are now inextricably linked in the consumer's mind with sinister culverts disgorging spates of industrial waste into dead lakes and rivers that catch fire. As a result, the once-buoyant image of the happy housewife plunged elbow-deep in suds has acquired such uncongenial undertones that advertisers have been forced to develop a more ecologically sensitive way of depicting the invisible process of cleaning: the old-fashioned soap bubble, which was pink, viscous, and semi-opaque, has given way to the new modern bubble, which is transparent and colorless. Moreover, old-fashioned suds were invariably depicted in a fleecy cloud that erupted out of sinks and washing machines, whereas contemporary bubbles travel alone, are relatively sparse, and, when represented at all, are often suspended in a wholesome-looking green fluid, replete with nurturing agricultural associations. In an ecologically correct age like our own, the soap itself has been laundered, reconstrued as an invigorating form of carbonation rather than as septic lather, thus severing subliminal connections of detergents with illegal spigots gushing effluents into aquifers.

While the aesthetic of cleanness usually operates by inventing sensual qualities for a state that has none, it also deliberately plays upon the imperceptibility of something it prefers us to imagine and intuit rather than to see: bacteria. The spurious sensuality of the aesthetic is thus complemented by its strategic use of the nonsensual, the invisible, the spectral threat that pervades the harmless-looking kitchen counter, which is in fact a petri dish swarming with staphylococcus and spirochetes, as in an ad for Lysol that presents a wide-eyed toddler reaching for a doorknob booby-trapped with pathogens: "One of the most dangerous things in your kitchen," the advertisement tells us, "may be something you can't even see." Similarly, Bounty, the Quilted Quicker Picker-Upper, shows a curious cherub standing before a counter on tippy toes about to snatch up a scouring pad marked with a warning as ominous as a skull and crossbones: "Pick up Bounty before somebody picks up a sponge full of germs." Cleanness is often a ghost story that instills alarm about an unspecified microbial menace, not by representing the threat but by toying with the elusiveness of the infinitesimal and thereby intensifying our fears of dangerous contaminants, much as tall tales told around campfires play upon the suggestiveness of empty rooms, showing us curtains that move, not who moved them, doors that slam, not who slammed them. The aesthetic of cleanness thus works in two contradictory ways: It endows nonphysical states with a superabundance of sensual qualities and it dwells upon the invisibility of things that are indeed real, conjuring up putatively normal kitchens that are actually death traps ready to ambush our offspring, who sicken and waste away from unseen hazards breeding on the knobs of our Kenmores and Hotpoints.

If bubbles have become cleaner and bacteria more threatening, skin has become more vulnerable. It is now described according to a new aesthetic that functions as a bizarre sort of meat tenderizer for a paper-thin pelt that is constantly wrinkling, scarring, spotting, cracking, and breaking out into patches of acne. Early in the twentieth century, it was still possible to find advertisements for lye soap that could be used for either cleaning one's clothing or washing one's face, or for Zonite, a "non-toxic," "non-caustic," "non-burning" mouthwash that was so versatile that it could be used both for gargling and for scrubbing bathroom sinks, for shampooing hair and de-grouting shower stalls. In the nineteenth century, the distinction between organic and inorganic surfaces was far less categorical than it is in an age in which the face is portrayed as such a fragile ornament that only the most advanced techniques of dermatological conservation will keep it from shriveling up like a prune or developing double chins and pendulous jowls. Through the rhetoric of the cosmetics industry, consumerism grafts onto our bodies a second skin, a hypothetical membrane so soft, so easily damaged, that plain old soap has become altogether taboo, replaced by scientifically engineered "sanitizing systems" that "cleanse" rather than "clean," that protect, soothe, and mollify rather than corrode and cauterize, such as Dove's Sensitive Skin Moisturizing Body Wash, which "is not a soap" but "a soap-free formula." The portrayal of skin as a permeable substance has led to the false specialization of cleaning products and the extinction of such unthinkably adaptable commodities as Zonite, which emerged from a culture still capable of seeing the body as just another inert object, subject to the same slow descent into rusty dilapidation as our stoves and wringer washers. As the distinction between the organic and the inorganic became absolute in the course of the twentieth century and a separate aesthetic of morbid vulnerability was invented for skin, soap suddenly went upscale and was diversified into a plethora of "cleansing" formulae and "spa concepts" that "hydrate," "anti-oxidize," and "nourish," acting as taxidermic agents on an artificially sickly substance that seems to serve no protective function whatsoever but is as easily bruised and perforated as the delicate tissues inside of our bodies.

This same hypochondriacal aesthetic of the disintegrating human pelt, whose "moisture-retaining lipid barrier" can be protected only by rubbing it with "extra-strength emollients and humectants," is now even being extended to porcelain and enamel fixtures, which must contend not only with the ravages of ring-around-the-tub and "waxy yellow build-up" but also with the damage of scouring pads and carbolic acids that scrape, scratch, and erode "today's beautiful surfaces," unlike Soft Scrub, which "kill[s] bacteria without killing your tub." The neo-natal delicacy of the models featured in advertisements for Estee Lauder's Multi-Action Complex or ReJuveness, which cures "hypertrophic and keloid scars," has been transferred to our sinks and floors, which are described as organisms whose "complexions" will become "sallow" unless they receive "the modern 'beauty treatment' for today's brilliant baths." The adaptability of cleaning products has been compromised, first by creating two separate and irreconcilable realms of the organic and the inorganic and then by paradoxically conflating the two, transforming the bathtub into a beleaguered odalisque who, like our "sleek new silky soft" hands and faces, must be "caressed" and "pampered" by a homemaker who functions less as a janitor than as a masseuse. Consumerism extends the metaphor of flesh to plastic, Lucite, Teflon, and tile and then creates new commodities that will be "gentle," "kind," "careful," and "whisper-soft" to cupboards and countertops that now demand from the housewife a fictional new level of diligence and caution to prevent dermatological disasters on sensitive toilet seats and nonstick skillets.

The new metaphors of cleanness work both ways, for if linoleum has become flesh, flesh has become linoleum. Manufacturers of antiperspirants in particular concoct a skin-substitute that mimics other synthetic household substances, whose dryness, durability, and stainlessness we have come to depend on. Advertisements for products like Ban, Mum, and Lady's Speed Stick create a sci-fi image of a plastic armpit, a

243

type of prosthetic hinge that neither sweats nor smells but offers all of the water-repellent features of Formica. At the same time that consumerism conjures up images of artificially soft skin, it also fabricates a fantastic vision of an unnaturally hard body, a Teflon mannequin that embodies a dream of futuristic efficiency, as easily sprayed, wiped, and cleaned as a toaster or a microwave. This inorganic cyborg finds one of its most immodest expressions in commercials in which models obscenely bare their naked, depilated pits, defiantly holding them up to the camera for inspection in a way that is only slightly less exhibitionistic than the vixens who sprawl spread-eagled in pornographic magazines. The "underarm," to use the expression advertisers still bashfully prefer over the more uncouth "armpit," was the first taboo part of a woman's body to be represented in advertising, as in the case of Dew Deodorant, which throughout the 1920s featured on its bottle a simple line drawing of a figure in a sleeveless negligee exposing to us an area so forbidden that it was once euphemistically known as "the curve beneath a woman's arm." Far from being sexual in appeal, these seemingly salacious images of women lolling about bewitchingly, their arms thrown up over their heads, inviting the photographer to poke his nose into their bald, sapless pits, are in fact utterly sexless. They depict a consumer who has been liberated from her own excretions and achieved an ideal state of inhuman desiccation, proudly triumphing over her own messy physiology to become a kitchen counter in a dress, a large, unperforated surface with no pores and no orifices.

Our confused and contradictory obsession with surfaces has been intensified by the radical changes that have occurred in the appearance of our houses in the course of the last hundred years. Virtually every object we own is now potentially a mirror, from our stainless steel convection ovens and our polished floors to our dinner plates ("I can see myself") and our flatware (a tiny image of an ecstatic bride and groom is reflected on the knife blade featured in one advertisement). Before the twentieth century, we lived in a world of unreflective surfaces, of flagstone floors and dark armoires that absorbed rather than transmitted the intermittent light cast by kerosene lamps that created at best small pools of incandescence hemmed in by shadows. The blazing hall of mirrors in which we now live has dramatically changed the way we perceive dirt, producing an omnipresent shine whose radiance is easily dulled by rust, abrasions, and patches of grime. When our eyes pass over a reflective surface, a lackluster smudge leaps out at us, whereas it tended to merge with its surroundings when most things were made out of wood or stone, materials now gilded with synthetic laminates that make everything as smooth as a billiard ball. This punitive new patina conscripts housewives in an endless war against the forces that tarnish the shellacked surfaces of rooms in which even the slightest diminishment of their bright, coercive luster triggers our instinct to clean. The pictorial convention in advertisements of the flashing star, the burst of celestial light that bounces like a streak of lightning off the mop in a commercial for linoleum floors or detonates on the crystal goblet drawn on the label of a dish detergent, is the fascist symbol of the new religion of shininess, whose disciples expend untold hours burnishing their acquisitions, coating them with polyurethane, rubbing them with Johnson's Wax, and polishing them with Lemon Pledge and Endust. New nonporous surfaces like enamel and plastic may be easy to clean, being free of crevices that catch dust, but they also must be cleaned more often to preserve easily dulled glazes that do not hide dirt but advertise it, making every spill, every stain, every spot painfully conspicuous.

Just as we have become the votaries of dazzling surfaces, so we have become the zealots of another mystery cult, the cult of the stain. Our phobia of spots is so intense that *Family Circle* magazine even maintains a twenty-four-hour "stain hotline" where trained counselors, like volunteers for the Samaritans, offer emergency telephone support to people heartbroken over that "early morning coffee spill on your new skirt." Similarly, the manufacturer of Shout Wipes encourages a mild form of agoraphobia by telling consumers never to "go out without your Shout," a disposable, stain-removing cloth that spares consumers the humiliation of arriving at work splattered like a Jackson Pollock with a hastily consumed breakfast. The laundry detergent industry bombards us with images of mythically radiant clothing that emerges from the drier, framed in a messianic aureole of light, the whites "whiter than white," the colors so bright they "bloom." Our indoctrination with pictures of preternaturally clean clothing, as if fresh from the store, has drastically reduced the life span of our wardrobes, which must be replaced long before the fabric even begins to fray, so intolerant have we become of even the slightest blemish on otherwise pristine garments. Whereas in the nineteenth century both the rich and the poor were more accustomed to seeing stains on clothing, which was replaced only when it was threadbare and hence was probably covered with splotches of coal soot and mud splashed from carriage wheels, we have grown habituated to vivid colors whose brightness has become a new source of obsolescence that leads to the intemperate consumption of textiles. Paradoxically, as we have seen in the case of quaintness, stains create "character" in furniture but they impugn it in clothing, reflecting negatively on the habits and integrity of the wearer, who is judged derelict in her hygienic duties, stigmatized as a careless slattern.

It is because our culture assigns allegorical meanings of rectitude to the state of stainlessness that carefully planned violations of the aesthetic of cleanness can be used as a form of rebellion, a way of flaunting one's difference from the pack, of advertising one's subversiveness. Slovenliness has become a form of political speech, the act of wearing artfully ripped clothing a puerile type of protest for those incapable of confronting the status quo through more direct methods of civil disobedience. So ineffective are the politics of the stain, so fundamentally unthreatening to the stability of our culture, that clothing companies like the Gap and Levi-Strauss even manufacture pre-torn, pre-faded, and pre-scuffed jeans, T-shirts, and tennis shoes for those who seek to rock the boat aesthetically, wearing a ready-made wardrobe of protest placards that cater to a market that confuses visual violations of decorum with political ones. The seditiousness of this new commercial niche is undermined by the fact that its rags are almost always freshly laundered, having come out of the same drier as Father's Brooks Brothers business shirts, Mother's conservative white blouses, and a "time-released" sheet of "the invigorating freshness of Bounce." Like the hipster's sonic vandalism, which registers dissidence through dissonance, cranking up the volume but respecting property, so the aesthetic vandalism of the stain is a harmless form of rebellion. The taboo against uncleanness is ultimately inviolable and can only be tested through symbolic transgressions that never risk the ostracism that would result from wearing clothing permeated with the stench of B.O.

Throughout the twentieth century, the aesthetic of cleanness has been simultaneously militaristic and ladylike. The rhetoric of germ warfare infuses descriptions of cleaning products, which depict housewives as soldiers on the front lines, "killing dirt," "cutting through stains," or "getting brutal with soiled clothing," as in an advertisement for Gain detergent that shows a laundress in a boxing glove clutching a pair of men's underwear ("Give your boxers some punch"); or in Procter & Gamble's classic advertisements for the "grime fighter" Mr. Clean, a muscle-bound pirate who, like a policeman, "arrests your dirt problem," knocking out grease with one fist and leaving a shine with the other. This saber-rattling of broomsticks and dust mops introduces narrative excitement into the drudgery of housework, transforming janitorial duties into an epic battle between an evil empire and a warrior princess, a virago who annihilates such foes as ring-around-the-collar and "those stubborn stains" that require "the added muscle" of Comet cleanser to make your house "company clean." Such hawkishness becomes more integral to the aesthetic of cleanness as housework becomes simpler and less time-consuming and women's confidence about the value of their domestic activities begins to wane. Consumerism compensates psychologically for the diminishment of women's historic custodial roles by reassuring them that, far from being mere squeezers of spray nozzles, pushers of self-cleaning oven buttons, and flickers of switches on garbage disposals, they are crackshot marksmen wielding potentially toxic, high-tech smart bombs. This martial aesthetic emerges only as women's roles begin to evolve beyond that of the nineteenth-century washerwoman, who had an unchallengeable sense of her own value and who therefore didn't need to be told that she was a commando in a hygienic crusade, a jihad against "greasy build-ups" and "those creepy, odor-causing germs."

This lank-haired charwoman, her hands covered with calluses and chilblains, is the subtext of most cleaning advertisements from the first half of the twentieth century, which portray housewives as exemplars of daintiness and good taste, aristocrats who sought to dissociate themselves from the chores of the scullery maid. Manufacturers emphasized that their products would enable these women to save precious time for social engagements and, moreover, would spare them the disfiguring effects of house cleaning on skin unaccustomed to the indignities of labor. Companies created props for a Little Lady fantasy about imaginary duchesses who seldom crawled around on all fours, their heads stuck in toilet bowls, but maintained their feminine dignity as useless ornaments who affected a pose of patrician uninvolvement from such tasks as washing windows and scouring pots and pans. Over time, manufacturers invented ways of keeping the cleaner clean, of sparing her the ordeal of wallowing in grime, thus enabling her to remain immaculate even in the midst of sordid jobs in which, in magazine advertisements, she is shown in all of her manicured, well-coifed splendor, darting about the room joyfully flicking her feather duster over her family photographs and porcelain figurines. The whole experience of cleaning has been redesigned in the course of the twentieth century so that we ourselves don't become dirty, the result in part of developments in cleaning products, most of which are disposable and do not themselves need to be cleaned, from "comfy-soft" paper towels and Sure & Natural Maxishields to Kleenex ColdCare tissues ("the yuck stops here") and Pampers that "clean perfect little tushies perfectly."

The aesthetic revolution of cleaning the cleaner can be seen in two small yet significant changes. First, advertisers now prefer to use the word "wipe" instead of "scrub," characterizing the act of cleaning not as a grueling expenditure of elbow grease but as an effortless dab with a "thirsty" paper towel which, in an almost imperceptible change of agency, does our work for us, sucking up spills, "loosening dirt," and "lifting out stains." Second, manufacturers have created containers that place as much distance as possible between the consumer and the cleaning fluid, which was first poured from bottles, then squirted, and is now misted by atomizers that allow us to remain dry, thus protecting our aesthetic integrity.

Political strides in women's rights were not the sole incentive behind manufacturers' efforts to simplify housework and create the leisure time that emancipated an entire class of menial slaves for more intellectual occupations in the workforce. The ideologically retrograde fantasy of the white-gloved Little Lady, who abhorred getting her hands wet and ruining her outfits, has also had a significant impact on women's lives, providing companies with the economic motivation to streamline chores that compromised the consumer's lofty affectations of matronly dignity. Social change often inadvertently originates in fantasies that are in themselves anything but progressive, as in the case of this game of aristocratic priggishness, which inspired inventions that liberated the housewife from the kitchen and enabled her to choose occupations outside of the conventional callings of maid and nanny.

Not only has the cleaner herself been aestheticized, but containers are now being designed as full-fledged ornaments, made from tastefully colored plastics in curvilinear shapes that blend inconspicuously into a room's decor. This new attention to the aesthetics of the bottle reflects the continued feminization of house-cleaning, whose utensils have been manufactured to look like vases or cut-glass decanters suitable for display out in the open on cosmetics tables rather than hidden away beneath kitchen sinks where we store ugly tubs of bleach and aerosol cans of oven cleaner. What's more, containers are increasingly transparent and glow like stained-glass windows when light passes through their blue and green fluids, an effect that is not only visually appealing but reassuring to the consumer, who is allowed to see inside of mysteriously opaque bottles that otherwise look like toxic drums of hazardous waste. Once again, our consciousness of pollution and our fear of ingesting carcinogens and other noxious substances have created a dilemma that manufacturers circumvent aesthetically by producing attractively vitreous bottles that conceal nothing and thus allay our suspicions about their harmfulness.

A somewhat opposite development has occurred in the evolution of the historic image of the bather who, in contemporary advertising, is not meant to be admired as a work of art, a decorative bauble, but as a human being in her own right. The aesthetic of cleanness has always used stereotypes of women as harem girls who luxuriate in their bathtubs, intoxicated by the oils they are constantly massaging into their skin, their lips parted in ecstasy. In the course of the twentieth century, images of the bathing odalisque, so pivotal to both Western art and advertising, have become as politically problematic as soap suds, associated as they are with women's intellectual subordination, their trivialization as mindless creatures of the flesh who are forever grooming their bodies, combing their seductive tresses, and submerging themselves in the "sultry, Polynesian passion" of Frangipani's Foam Bath or Calgon's Berry Bliss, which promises "a divinely decadent dip into indulgence." In an effort to avoid offending the political sensitivities of our time, the age-old sensualist, as languorous as a figure in an Ingres painting, has been recast in the image of the liberated self-seeker who "takes time out" for rest and relaxation and uses bathing as a means of "pampering" herself, as "water therapy," a ritual for winding down after a harrowing day at the office. Whereas the old-fashioned odalisque used bathing as a means of preparing her body to be used by men, the new corporate odalisque immerses herself in soothing sea salts and packs on mud facials as an expression of her autonomy and self-respect, her desire to escape from the pressure of her family and job, and "to be nice to *You* for a change." In this way, Madison Avenue has craftily updated the venerable motif of the orgasmic bather, submerged to her eyebrows in "creamy lather as velvety as the petals of a rose," and created instead a liberated hydrotherapist who has rejected her passivity to men. While this change may put a flattering spin on women's compulsion to preen, it carefully preserves the economic status quo of the soap industry, which continues to exploit the stereotype of women as prisoners of their bathrooms, aquatic captives shackled to their sinks, steeping in tubs and reveling in the "softly sublime summer of renewal" contained in a fruit-scented "splash."

If women have become self-pamperers, children have become outright monsters. Innocent cherubs smeared with their mother's lipstick, covered head to toe in strawberry jam, splashing in puddles, and leaving circles of wet footprints on the living room carpet are the demented mascots of cleaning advertisements, which playfully evoke the exasperation parents feel about enfants terribles who fingerpaint elegant homes with swirls of spaghetti sauce and chocolate syrup. Every blank surface is a potential canvas for these lurking abstract expressionists, who run to the refrigerator the moment Mother's back is turned, as in the advertisement for Armstrong linoleum that shows a child sitting on a floor, surrounded by squirts of mustard, hand prints of peanut butter, and globs of whipped cream. Although advertisements that feature kids wreaking havoc in the house are intended to portray the laughable tribulations of child-rearing, they nevertheless express genuine hostility towards creatures who deface our property, undoing hours of arduous labor within seconds. By universalizing the experience of infantile messiness and offering the consumer a kind of collective wink, advertisers defuse our paroxysms of rage. Moreover, they implicitly characterize themselves as our saviors, as therapists who keep us from beating brats soaked with mud to a bloody pulp by coming to our res-

cue with paper towels whose "super strength and ab-
sorbency will clean up the whole mess completely,"
thereby allowing us to deal with "the inevitable reality of
having children." It is always the advertiser who cleans
up the pigsty, always the spot remover that "lifts out" the
bright purple grape juice spill, never the adult, who sits
idly by letting Brillo and Fantastic do all of the work.
Manufacturers use their advertisements to stimulate two
contradictory emotions: the fierce maternalism we feel
for children who are shown in that archetypal "Kodak
moment," looking adorably sheepish beneath an overturned plate of pasta, and the lunatic frenzy that comes
over us when we see our perfectly scrubbed floors black-
ened with scuff marks and that expensive Osh Kosh
B'Gosh outfit sticky with ice cream and chocolate cake.
After turning us into child beaters, advertisers calmly
offer a solution, presenting themselves as aerosol genii
in spray cans capable of placating our homicidal impulses by taking on their own shoulders all of the re-
sponsibility for cleaning up the disaster.

Like deliciousness, whose exaggerated rhetorical
mannerisms were specifically designed to address problems pertaining to the packaging of food in the last 150
years, cleanness also addresses a peculiarly modern

predicament: messiness, a phenomenon that differs significantly from dirtiness. The latter is an age-old problem, but messiness occurs only in a culture that owns too many things, that subscribes to too many newspapers, collects too many pairs of shoes, buys too many coats, and hence is constantly fighting the battle of ever-diminishing storage space. We are drowning in a rising tide of unnecessary acquisitions that choke our tiny apartments, inhibit our mobility, and oppress us aesthetically, despite the ingenious efforts of the new space-control industry, which has redesigned our rooms to take advantage of every available square inch, offering such devices as shoe racks that unfold like accordions and spinning carousels for ties and belts. If deliciousness helps us deal with the revulsion we feel from the tastelessness of processed foods, cleanness helps reduce anxiety about owning more things than we can possibly store. The punishingly esoteric art of household organization is intended, not as a cure, but as a form of damage control that dissuades us from taking the ultimate solution to clutter, to stop buying altogether, an economically catastrophic decision that manufacturers prevent us from making by encouraging us to empty out our rooms, which are no sooner stripped bare than they immediately fill up again, reverting to their natural state of anarchic squalor.

If cleanness provides a psychological placebo for mess, another technique for encouraging consumption in the age of bursting closets is to blame the victim, to describe clutter as if it were not the outcome of compulsive acquisitiveness but of the weak character of the owner, whom we are taught to believe is a slob, a pack rat who obsessively hoards every piece of string and pencil stub he acquires. According to this view, clutter is not the result of the fact that we buy more things than we have room for but of the moral failing of the consumer, who is shamed into feeling undisciplined and careless, whereas in fact the cyclical decline of our rooms into a state of disarray is a symptom of our psychological maladjustment to the overabundance of consumerism. Blaming the victim spares the manufacturer, who photographs his products in austere and immaculate settings. The "'less-is-more' mindset" encouraged by the home economics movement produces intimidatingly pristine modernist cubes, the ascetic centerfolds in *Architectural Digest* and *House Beautiful,* whose unfurnished spareness further contributes to our sense of guilt and constriction, of being hemmed in by piles of rubbish. The feeling of congestion that we are indoctrinated to believe is the result of our own shortcomings leads to feverish bouts of spring cleaning as we jettison things we are convinced we are too scatterbrained to organize, making fruitless efforts to overcome our deficiencies as homemakers and recreating our rooms in the ubiquitous image of uninhabitably deserted interiors that beckon us with wide open spaces enticingly free of refuse.

Cleanness is such a crucial aesthetic to consumerism because it is the very mechanism that keeps us buying, that controls the flow of commodities in and out of our houses and thus numbs us to the irritation of overcrowding. We live in a culture of trash, one that discards as much as it acquires, a binge-and-purge culture in which the accusatory minimalism of cleanness functions as nothing less than an emetic. Throwing things out is the reverse side of consuming, the Shiva principle of capitalism, the spirit of destruction without which there could be no creation, no production.

AFTERWORD

T hroughout this book, I have shown how the aesthetics of consumerism are the lies we tell ourselves to preserve our individuality even as we enjoy the luxuries of the mass market. An afterword is an appropriate place to examine my own position within this scheme, to lay my cards out on the table, and, because I am so sensitive to the lies of others, ask what lies I am telling myself, what deceptions may lurk behind my own stance as a scold, the captious conscience of consumerism. Am I too another victim of the seductive illusions of what I have identified as controlled nonconformity? Do I too believe, in my heart of hearts, that I have somehow transcended the system of which I am inevitably a part, that I too am a rebel, an oddball? While I do not drive a fast car (or any car at

263

all for that matter) or wear ostensibly "unique" clothing or pretend that I am a crazy, lovable misfit, do I not
still believe that I have preserved my individuality by
setting myself up as my culture's gadfly, the scourge of
the store shelf and the cineplex? Perhaps my entire
book is nothing more than an intellectual's tribute to
the aesthetic of zaniness, to controlled nonconformity,
to every consumer's frustrated desire to stand out from
the crowd, whether it be by wearing a squirting carna-
tion in his lapel, dying his hair green, piercing his
tongue and septum, or writing a poison pen account of
the magnificent vulgarity of capitalism.

After reading a book as critical as mine, people often
expect the author to propose a constructive alternative
and translate his objections into a concrete agenda for
social change, the blueprint of an ideal society to replace
the one he has contemptuously disavowed. As a cultural
critic and not a visionary or prophet, I have always felt
that it is sufficient for me to destroy—to slash, to burn—
and have never felt any desire to formulate utopian so-
lutions, not only because I wish to avoid blunting the full
force of my skepticism and palliating my reader's urgent
need for happy endings, but because I frankly do not
have any answers to offer, no five-year plan, no program

for reform, no campaign for organizing the Great Leap Forward into paradise on Earth.

What, after all, would a world without consumerism be like? Surely not one that I myself would choose to live in. There would be no cities because cities are dependent on trade, nor money because there would be nothing to buy. There would be no insurance companies because there would be no possessions, no realtors because there would be no houses, no lawyers because hunters and gatherers rarely have to untangle the red tape of copyright infringement or haggle over joint stock agreements or fax each other angry letters to cease and desist. To imagine a world without consumerism is to erase oneself, to devolve through eons of human progress back to an era in which all of our time would have been devoted to scrabbling in the dust for roots and berries, with not a second to spare for making art or reading literature, let alone for writing ungrateful diatribes attacking the very society that has made my life and its manifold comforts possible.

Daniel Harris

ACKNOWLEDGMENTS

I t is a truism of the literary profession that the writer leads a solitary life, and, in most respects, my own experience bears this out. I have been extremely lucky, however, to share my cork-lined room with a number of other recluses who have diligently commented on the blizzard of manuscripts in which I buried them in the course of writing this book.

Most important, I would like to thank my lover, John MacLaren, for his intelligence, tact, patience, sense of humor, and . . . I could go on but only at the risk of making my reader jealous. John is an historian of ancient art, a designer of beautiful furniture, and, that rarest of things, an aesthete devoid of pretensions—rarer still, of cash. He was thus the ideal companion for a project dealing with the aesthetics of the marketplace.

Amelia Arenas, a brilliant essayist, lecturer, cultural critic, historian, curator, and, much as she despises the term, crusading art "educator," has also provided me with abundant criticism and support.

Joaquin Martinez-Pizarro still has not learned to write "good" anywhere in the margins of my manuscripts. I overlook this ghastly shortcoming only because he is so astute in his criticisms and, since he is dependably frugal with his praise, so credible. I rely on his support, encouragement, and shrewd suggestions more than he will ever know.

Julia Foulkes, a talented historian at the New School, was also generous enough to read my manuscripts at a moment's notice. She provided many constructive criticisms (as well as a number of destructive ones that ultimately made a great deal of sense after I had the chance to lick my wounds).

As always, I would like to thank my former lover Anthony Aziz and his current companion Sammy Cucher for their loyalty and friendship. Life wouldn't be the same without these two tremendous friends.

Several editors have also played a key role in encouraging me during this project, most important my own editor at Basic Books, John Donatich, who—

unlike some—does write "good" in the margins of my manuscript and also provides superb advice on passages that he is tactful enough not to condemn outright as "bad." As always, I would also like to thank Robert and Peggy Boyers, the editors of *Salmagundi,* where most of my pieces appear. They have been unflaggingly loyal to me over the years. Without their constant support and encouragement, generously underwritten by Skidmore College, I would have stopped writing long ago. I would also like to thank Ann Fadiman at *The American Scholar* and Robert Fogarty at *The Antioch Review.* My agent, Malaga Baldi, has been a model of patience. She has worked indefatigably on my behalf and talked me through many discouraging moments.

The staff at my day job in the word processing center of the law firm Fish & Neave also deserves a big round of applause. Three writers, an operatic soprano, two baritones, a jazz singer, a librettist, an actor, a recent Ph.D., an occupational therapist, a stand-up comic, and several other amazingly good-natured people (including the fabulous Bessie Anderson and Liz Tan) have made my stay there a real pleasure. With the NEA in shambles, law firms are the last patrons of the arts and I am grateful to Fish & Neave for respecting my odd scheduling needs.

I would also like to thank my landlady, Marie Librera, her daughter Vanessa Librera, and Vanessa's son Joseph Marler, none of whom have ever had their names in a book before. They are three of the most gracious people I have known.